BISCUITS

BISCUITS

SWEET AND SAVORY SOUTHERN RECIPES FOR THE ALL-AMERICAN KITCHEN

Jackie Garvin

Skyhorse Publishing

Skyhorse Publishing books may be purchased in bulk at special discounts for sales promotion, corporate gifts, fund-raising, or educational purposes. Special editions can also be created to specifications. For details, contact the Special Sales Department, Skyhorse Publishing, 307 West 36th Street, 11th Floor, New York, NY 10018 or info@skyhorsepublishing.com.

Skyhorse® and Skyhorse Publishing® are registered trademarks of Skyhorse Publishing, Inc.®, a Delaware corporation.

Visit our website at www.skyhorsepublishing.com.

10 9 8 7 6 5 4 3 2

Library of Congress Cataloging-in-Publication Data

Garvin, Jackie.
  Biscuits : sweet and savory Southern recipes for the all-American kitchen / Jackie Garvin.
      pages cm
  Includes bibliographical references and index.
  ISBN 978-1-63220-347-2 (alk. paper) -- ISBN 978-1-63450-008-1 (ebook) 1. Biscuits.
2. Cooking, American--Southern style. I. Title.
  TX770.B55G37 2015
  641.81'57--dc23
                                    2015005151

Print ISBN: 978-1-63220-347-2
Ebook ISBN: 978-1-63450-008-1

Printed in China

In memory of my grandparents, Payton (1902–1992)
and Virginia (1907–1990) Phillips, whose unfaltering
love showed me the way to peace and grace.

John 14:27

Contents

Acknowledgments

To my husband, Sam: Finding your soul mate is a blessing and I have been abundantly blessed to share my life with you over the past forty years. Our married life has been rich, sweet, fulfilling and, at times, sad. The rich blessings we received at the moment we first laid eyes on each of our three babies will carry us through the rest of our lives. Watching those sweet babies grow into responsible, caring, loving adults is the grand prize of parenting. We've gently caressed each other's broken hearts and shared the sadness when we had to say goodbye to loved ones. Our travels have taken us on fun, exciting, and interesting excursions. My heart would swell each time I saw the pride on your face when you talked to someone about my cookbook. I'm undeserving of such loyalty and love but eternally grateful.

To my children, Marcia, Amy, and Tyler: I'm so proud of each of you. You've brought an immeasurable amount of joy and love into my life. I give thanks to God for you every day. Thank you for your encouragement and interest in this project.

To my son-in-law, David: You're a wonderful addition to our family. Thank you for being such a loving husband to my daughter and father to my grandchildren. Your support of this project means a tremendous amount to me.

To my grandchildren, Jackson and Ella: I hope you'll be proud of Nana's book one day and that it will help you understand a little bit more about your Southern heritage.

To my friends, Dawn, Shari, and Myrna: I've leaned on each of you in different ways and you never let me down. Such friendship is a rare commodity and I can't adequately thank you for all you've done. You've been there with me every step of the way.

To my editor, Nicole Frail: You were the driving force behind this book and held the hand of this novice author throughout the process. You were editor, psychologist, cheerleader, and advocate. Thank you for believing in me.

To my publisher, Skyhorse Publishing: Thank you for taking a chance on me.

To all the members of Buckhorn Springs Golf and Country Club: Thank you for your willing acceptance of our many offerings of biscuits.

To all the friends who I know in person or who follow me on various social media outlets: You have been so sweet and kind to me. Your notes, emails, and comments keep my spirits lifted, my motivation high, and my belief in the goodness of people alive. Y'all are the reason Syrup and Biscuits continues.

To Kurt Halls: your constant quest to be good and do right inspires me.

To Becky and Mary Pat: not only are you top notch personal trainers and fitness experts, but you are my inspiration to stay on track and healthy. Thank you for taking a personal interest in my crazy, wild aspirations.

To my fellow Stephen Ministers at St. Andrew's United Methodist Church, Brandon, Florida: You have lifted me up and given me inspiration. God works through each of you. Thank you for sharing your loving hearts with me.

To my sisters, Kathy and Sue: You will always be a part of my story.

To my mother-in-law, Dorothy Garvin: You've supported me in everything I've ever attempted. I hope you enjoy sharing this cookbook with your friends.

My Biscuit Heritage

A baby born to teenage parents—parents who had no advantages, no education beyond high school, low paying jobs, and no prospect of higher earnings whose own parents were former tenant farmers—isn't usually destined for greatness. In fact, that baby has a lot of odds stacked against her. How that baby was able to thrive, meet and marry her soul mate, get an education, raise a family, achieve every professional goal she set, and eventually land a contract to write a book is either the stuff from which fairy tales are made or simply an example of the power of traditional Southern values such as faith, family, respect, hard work, honesty, and lots of good homegrown tomatoes. My story is the former. Who's to say how much of a role homegrown tomatoes actually played, but I know the important role and impact of Southern values in my life. *Southerner* is as much a part of my identity as *woman, wife, mother, sister, aunt, grandmother, friend,* and *neighbor.* It's more than an identifier; it's a component of my DNA. I live in the South and the South lives in me. I willingly and proudly accept, admit, and display it.

My birth at Fort Rucker, Alabama, in 1955, added another generation of Alabamians to a multi-generational Alabama lineage. That lineage continued for one more generation with the birth of my daughters in Mobile. With Alabamians above and below me in my ancestral line, and all around me in everyday life, the connection to biscuits is obvious. Biscuits were as common as air and almost as necessary.

So many of the good things in life, the things that really matter, came to me by way of an un-assuming cotton mill village in the small southeastern town of Geneva, Alabama. That's where my parents grew up and both sets of my grandparents lived. I only lived in Geneva a few years, but I certainly spent a lot of time there during the summers with my mother's parents, Payton and Virginia

Phillips. If you noticed a few pages back, I dedicated this book to their memory, which indicates the profound impact they had on my life and my view of the world.

As I reflect on precious memories from Geneva, I keep going back to the familiar scene of shelling peas on the front porch. We either picked the peas or Granny and Granddaddy bought them. They would buy them by the hamperful. Despite a valiant effort, I'm unable to find a weight equivalent for a hamper of peas. Take my word for it when I say it's *a lot*. Shelling a hamper of peas takes a long time. Sometimes, they'd buy two at a time. My sisters and I were given small enamelware bowls that we filled up with unshelled peas; we'd shell until our fingers almost fell off. Granny and Granddaddy brought out large dishpans for themselves. The shelling lasted into the night.

When my sisters and I grew tired of shelling, we took breaks and climbed the Chinaberry tree that grew so close to the house, we could reach it from the porch. Citronella candles were lit to keep mosquitoes from taking us off. As we shelled, talk would drift in and out with multiple topics that displayed the simple, down home lifestyle of our Geneva family and friends. Subjects like Aunt Mary's chickens and the slop buckets Uncle Preston hung around for folks to discard leftover food he would feed to the chickens always seemed to make their way into conversation. We would perk up when a possible trip to Sandy Creek, a favorite swimming hole, was mentioned. People drove by and waved. We waved back. Then either Granny or Granddaddy would announce the latest news they knew about the driver of the car. Granny, a seamstress, always discussed her current sewing projects. Granddaddy talked about who missed choir practice, who they needed to visit in the hospital, and who he just happened to run in to last time he went to town. Part of the conversation was devoted to who had fallen on hard times and needed help. Without exception, Granny detailed with whom she planned on sharing a prepared dish. Summers with my grandparents continued until my early teens when I reached the age wherein I thought spending weeks in Geneva was simply too boring.

Sundays in Geneva meant church twice a day. Early Sunday morning, the radio was turned to gospel music and we listened to The Florida Boys and The Happy Goodman Family as Granny cooked a big breakfast consisting of eggs, grits, biscuits, gravy, and either bacon or sausage. We dressed in our Sunday best and headed off to church. I loved seeing Granddaddy in the choir and hearing his booming baritone voice. We made sure to look for Miss Argo, who carried candy to pass out to children. Granny took out her Bible when it was time for scripture reading and always marked the date and the name of the preacher who read the passage. At night, we went back to church for Training Union.

Prior to the cotton mill, Geneva was a little town that never got much recognition unless the Pea River overgrew its banks and flooded the town. In July 1923, the Geneva Cotton Mill was organized by founders Jim Johnston, Sr. and D. H. Morris, Jr. The mill meant a boon to Geneva's shaky economy and offered steady work to citizens in and around Geneva County, who had few options other than tenant farming to earn a living. The work in the cotton mill was hard and hot, but it meant a steady paycheck and housing. The mill village, within walking distance of the mill, comprised three-room houses offered to the workers for rent so low it could have been considered a token gesture. The mill whistle blew to signal when it was time to wake up and, again when it was time to be at work. The whistle was heard throughout several counties and served as the official time clock. Residents of the mill village lived, worked, raised children, and worshipped together. They looked out after each other and lent a helping hand when needed. My observation of the mill people taught me how to relate to people and how to treat them. It was the genesis of my long-lasting faith in God. I learned that we all need to work hard, be good, and do right. Along with the economic boost, the mill brought a way of life grounded in Southern values and Judeo-Christian principles.

My family moved throughout Alabama until I was eight years old. At that time, we landed in Mobile where I remained until my husband and I moved our family, consisting of two daughters, to the Tampa, Florida, suburbs in 1985. Mobile was, and has remained, a Southern town with a Southern personality. Tampa is geographically further south than Mobile, but you have to go north to get back in the South. Our daughters were five and seven when we left Mobile and our son was born five years after we settled in Florida. I worked hard to ensure my children understood and appreciated their Southern heritage. At holidays, we observed our family traditions. I taught them the meaning and the stories of the few family heirlooms I possessed and encouraged them to read Southern literature and watch movies based in the South. Frequently, I reminded them of the hardscrabble lives of our ancestors and of our good fortune of many blessings. With the determination of Scarlett O'Hara, I vowed, with God as my witness, that my children would not become de-Southernized.

In the summer of 1996, we moved into our current home—a two-story Colonial farmhouse style with a wraparound porch situated on property that had been pasture land for the past one hundred

years with lots of grandfather oaks draped in Spanish moss in plain view. A kitchen of adequate size begged for lots of cooking. Landscape materials were carefully chosen to resemble the old South and not new Florida. Everything about our home, inside and out, felt right and familiar. Finally, I felt I was back in my beloved Deep South.

Excitedly, I jumped right in to banging pots and pans and turning out lots of good eats from my new kitchen. Amidst the happiness of gravy making, meat roasting, vegetable boiling and cobbler baking, a strange and hideous notion crept into my head. Disregarding it for as long as possible, I eventually gave way to the thought that down home Southern cooking was boring and uninteresting. I had to spread my wings and venture into the world of gourmet cooking. Paradoxically, I was now surrounded by more Southernness in my home than I had been for the past eleven years, but I was ready to forsake the one thing that had the closest ties to my Southern roots: down home Southern cooking. Southerners share their history, cultures, and traditions through food. So, without so much as a whimper, I bid farewell to my native cuisine.

The next few years were marked by collections of cookbooks and subscriptions to cooking magazines that would teach me how to cook gourmet and make our meals more interesting and appealing. My children found my experimental dishes fun, while my husband—a good ol' Southern boy with simple tastes—tolerated them. My collection of cookbooks and magazines was so extensive that I went a long time without cooking the same thing twice. How exciting! Or was it?

As my oldest daughter's twentieth birthday drew near, I happened upon one of Nathalie Dupree's cookbooks, *Southern Memories*. The cover photo is lovely with Nathalie sitting outside in a white wicker chair holding a glass of iced tea and sporting a bouffant hairstyle. The photo screamed, "Southern!" Briefly skimming the pages, I thought this would be a nice gift of authentic Southern recipes for my daughter, who would soon enter adulthood. I was four years into my gourmet cooking experience. Guilt pangs were tugging at my heart over the years lost to my departure from Southern cooking. I hoped this book would replace the teaching I hadn't done with my daughter.

Inside the cover, I wrote:

To Marcia,
Happy 20th Birthday.
Love, your family.

Once I sat down to read Nathalie's book, I couldn't stop until it was finished cover to cover. She told lovely stories of luncheons, parties, family gatherings, and life in the South. She reintroduced me to Southern cooking in a way that was exciting, colorful, and enticing. Nothing in the book was boring and uninteresting as I had painted Southern cooking four years ago. With the scales removed from my eyes, the prodigal daughter was ready to return home. My kitchen began cranking out Southern dishes again and it hasn't stopped. In Spring of 2014, I met Nathalie at a writer's workshop and told her the story.

I brought the book along, which she graciously autographed and wrote:

April 2014,
To Jackie who took this cookbook as her own!
Season with love – Nathalie Dupree

My professional career was neither food nor writing related. I was a Registered Nurse by training and went from Staff Nurse to Charge Nurse to Program Coordinator to Branch Manager to Area Director to Vice President to Entrepreneur within the Healthcare Industry. In December 2008, I successfully sold my healthcare-related company and worked for three months as a consultant to the buyer. In March 2009, I hung up my ballet slippers for good and retired. At fifty-three years old, I had too much energy and motivation to wake up every morning with an empty plate, so I dove headfirst into Bible studies and volunteer opportunities at my church. Since I had gotten that whole Southern food thing straightened out, I eagerly looked for opportunities to do something Southern-food-related in addition to the cooking I was doing at home. My daughter had given me a recipe organizer as a gift, and one of the first projects I undertook after retirement was organizing more than thirty years' worth of collected recipes. Then I cleaned out all my closets.

In February 2011, I mustered up enough courage to check out that new social media platform called Facebook. Not only was Facebook new to me, but so was social media. Surprisingly enough, I found so much of Facebook was intuitive for me and I took to it right away. I set up a personal profile and connected with friends and family, some of whom I hadn't seen or heard from in more than thirty years. With a respectable number of Facebook friends under my belt, I decided I would try my hand at writing—real food writing.

The first recipe I shared was a family favorite: Blackberry Cobbler. Along with the recipe, I wrote a narrative that described my summers in Geneva picking blackberries for my grandmother. People loved the recipe and left me so many sweet comments. To my surprise, they liked the narrative as much or maybe more than the recipe. They commented on how it brought back so many memories, how it made them cry, and how much they loved it. I tried my luck again to see if this was simply a fluke, and I got the same response and encouragements to continue writing. This seemed like the food connection for which I had been searching and a way to document my collection of recipes which were finally nicely organized and easily accessible.

I continued sharing my food writing posts on my personal Facebook profile. Someone suggested I start a "blog." After they explained to me what they meant by "blog," it sounded like something I wanted to do. First, I needed a name for my blog that was decidedly Southern and reflected something of importance in my life. I chose Syrup and Biscuits as a nod to memories of my grandparents and the breakfast that my Granddaddy ate every day of his life: cane syrup and biscuits. My learning curve for the blog platform was a little longer than it was for the Facebook platform, but I mastered it along with several social media platforms. A big chunk of my day was devoted to food writing and I thought I was in Heaven. Then, when I got an offer from D'Ann White to be a regular contributor to an online publication, I knew it *had* to be Heaven. I was honored and flattered and continued contributing weekly to The Patch, an AOL product, for a year.

My blog and social media followings continued growing at a pace that I thought only possible in my dreams. Constantly, I was able to preach the news about Southern food, food memories, family, faith, patriotism, and the goodness of people. My recipes and stories were featured on many sites throughout the Internet. Connecting with people, sharing the good news about my beloved South, and occasionally sneaking in photos of my grandchildren and Bassett Hound are so special to me. I found a way to honor my heritage, spread positive messages, and share the best the South has to offer: our food and culture. While I was happy with all that I was doing, I had a burning desire to write a cookbook. That shouldn't come as any great surprise. Anyone who has looked out their kitchen window as they wash dishes after a wonderful meal they've prepared wants to write a cookbook.

In November 2013, I received an email from Nicole Frail with Skyhorse Publishing. She asked me if I had considered writing a cookbook. She went on to say that her company was interested in a biscuit cookbook and wondered if I'd like to talk to them about it. I must have read that email twelve times to make sure I was reading it right. Just to be safe, I had my husband read it, too. It looks like I *was* reading it right.

In the traditional publishing world, it takes about eighteen months, start to finish, to publish a book. This book has taken me much longer than the usual amount of time; I've been working on it for fifty-nine years plus the seven or eight generations before me. It's up to me to represent and share the traditions, love, prayers, memories, and attitude of everything that's good and right about a Southern heritage. Every time we gather as family to bless a meal, I feel a connection to the generations before me who strived for a better life for their children and grandchildren. I'm compelled to honor my ancestors, who lived their lives in a kind of poverty that, thankfully, doesn't exist in this country today. When I think of Southern food and the recipes handed down many generations to me, the food doesn't seem boring and uninteresting at all. I see it as creative and brilliant. With no knowledge to speak of regarding nutrition, and even fewer financial resources, they knew how to sustain themselves in the most efficient way possible, make the food delectable, and create a desirable cuisine that's gained national popularity. That, my friends, is notable. I'm keenly aware that I didn't make it to where I am today on my own. I've been prayed for and prayed over.

So, here I am after finding my way, losing my way, and finding it again. I'm ready and able to put my Southern heritage on stage and tell y'all 'bout some biscuits.

My Biscuit Story

With a Southern heritage as rich as mine, it's not unreasonable to imagine that I learned to make biscuits before I learned to write. I have wonderful memories of my grandmother's daily routine of biscuit baking when she pulled out her biscuit bowl full of flour and knew just the right amount of unmeasured ingredients to produce consistently perfect biscuits. I loved grabbing bits of dough scraps to eat and hearing her say, "Don't eat too much o' that dough. It'll give you worms." Many times, too many to count, I've used biscuits to sop up cane syrup laden with soft butter. As far back as I remember, I've loved a biscuit stuffed with bacon. Yes, I've been surrounded by biscuits, eaten biscuits, loved biscuits, dreamed of biscuits my entire life, but I'm a living testimony that all that doesn't translate into biscuit baking prowess. I was a decades-long biscuit failure. As odd as it may seem, that's the reason you can rely on me to teach you biscuit-baking skills.

By the time I became interested in learning the art and technique of biscuit making, my grandmother was interested in shortcuts and had discovered the wonderment of canned biscuits. She thought they were a fine substitute and all I needed to know was how to crack open the can and be prepared for the *pop*. My mother, not an enthusiastic cook, didn't know how to make scratch biscuits herself. Off and on, throughout the years, I experimented with scratch biscuits and had every failure imaginable. At various times, my biscuits were hard, flat, burned, tasteless, or soggy. On occasion, they might have been all those at once. Without anyone to guide me, I never made progress. Batch after batch after sad, pitiful batch, my biscuits failed. Mind you, this was before the days of the Internet. Access to information wasn't nearly as easy as it is today. It never crossed my mind that the public library bought cookbooks and would have been a rich resource for biscuit-baking information. So, as far as I could tell, I was relegated to the art and technique of popping open canned biscuits. Hard as I tried, I could never help but jump when the can popped. When I discovered commercially prepared frozen biscuits, clearly superior to canned biscuits, I felt my quest for good biscuits was over once and for all.

After starting my blog, Syrup and Biscuits, I had the good sense to know that if I publish a blog with biscuit in the name, I'd better figure out how to include a biscuit recipe in an article. The thought caused me as much stress as an IRS audit. Having no confidence in my scratch biscuit making abilities and no mentor around, I relied on Bisquick to help me out of a jam. The baking mix was a staple in my pantry and I used it frequently for quick pancakes and, occasionally, casseroles. The directions for biscuits were right there on the box staring back at me. They were simple, straightforward, and had two ingredients: baking mix and milk. The first experiment was drop biscuits, which came out with a nice flavor, but I didn't like the appearance. They looked more like coconut macaroons than biscuits. With my courage up and my rolling pin in hand, I went for the gusto and produced rolled and cut biscuits, substituting buttermilk for sweet milk. They came out looking like biscuits and tasting like biscuits. I wrote up an article for the blog and called them **Easy Buttermilk Biscuits**. Now that I had an article and recipe for buttermilk biscuits on the blog, my work was done.

Time dragged on, my blog's readership grew, and I had overcome another big cooking hurdle. Along with the success of rolled and cut biscuits, I had mastered Chicken and Dumplings, another Southern kitchen iconic dish that resulted in failure after failure. You probably won't be surprised that I used the same Bisquick and buttermilk recipe for the dumplings as I did for the biscuits. As I continued to share my stories and recipes for authentic Southern cooking, a little voice kept coaxing me to do something about my biscuits. I answered the call with exhaustive research on scratch biscuit techniques. I read everything I could get my hands on and watched every YouTube video I could find about biscuits and took copious notes. I couldn't have been more focused, precise, and dedicated if I was conducting research to write a scholarly paper. After reviewing, rewriting, reviewing, and rewriting my notes, I was ready. With all the determination I could muster, I grabbed my mixing bowl, White Lily flour, butter, and buttermilk. My kitchen was a battle ground and I had no intention of surrendering to defeat.

After I put the first batch in the oven, I treated them as though they were one of my children admitted to the hospital: I never left their side and didn't take my eyes off them. Sitting on the floor in front of the stove peering in through the glass, I waited for the rise of the dough. And rise, they did! The first batch was perfect: tender, flaky, golden, and high.

Since my first good batch of scratch biscuits, I haven't had another biscuit failure. In fact, my technique has improved. I can make those biscuits so high, tender, and flaky, I surprise myself.

Decades of biscuit failure combined with exhaustive biscuit research has produced surefire techniques, tips, and knowledge that is reliable. I'm ready to share that knowledge with you and the world.

America's Biscuit History

I n 1606, the Susan Constant, Godspeed, and Discovery sailed from England with 144 men and boys from The Virginia Company of London with the New World as their destination. When they landed at Jamestown, Virginia, in spring 1607, they brought ashore items that were the precursor to modern American biscuits: hard tack biscuits (also called ships' biscuits), pigs, and cattle. Hard tack biscuits bear little resemblance to their progeny, the Southern iconic biscuit. They were durable, thin, hard, and tasteless. Made with flour and water, and sometimes salt, they could practically last forever if kept dry, making them a practical food source for long journeys.

My stated intention is not to minimize the hardships these early settlers faced or suggest that anybody during that time gave any consideration to transforming hard tack into a light fluffy biscuit. The history of our country's beginnings is fascinating. The entire timeline, from the establishment of the first permanent English colony at Jamestown in 1607, to our fight for independence, is filled with events and people deserving of the utmost respect and praise. The purpose of this narrative is simply to illustrate the history and transformation of American biscuits.

Once Jamestown was settled and the inhabitants planted crops, they discovered the warm climate of Virginia was suitable for growing a variety of wheat that made baked goods more tender. It was also discovered that the addition of lard from pigs and buttermilk from cows resulted in bread that could be made quickly, negating the need for yeast, which wasn't always available and required a long process to activate.

In the 1830s, bakers began adding sodium bicarbonate (baking soda) to dough to produce bubbles that were entrapped in the dough, creating a light bread. It was soon discovered that sodium bicarbonate in the presence of a light acid, produced even lighter bread. However, an exact ratio of sodium bicarbonate to acid, difficult to reproduce in kitchens, was necessary for consistent results. Biscuit bakers unable to obtain sodium bicarbonate initiated the practice of beaten biscuits. The biscuit dough

America's Biscuit History

was beaten with a hard object for about twenty to thirty minutes until the dough blistered and popped, signaling trapped air. This process resulted in softer, albeit flat, biscuits that resembled a soft cracker.

In 1856, German-trained Harvard chemist Eben Horsford received a patent for a powder that was a combination of sodium bicarbonate and a mild acid in the form of cream of tartar. Horsford along with his partner, George Wilson, created Rumsford Chemical Works to produce the necessary chemicals and proportions for calcium acid phosphate to replace cream of tartar, which was imported from Italy and France. Eventually, the product was packaged as Horsford's Bread Preparation, but the chemicals had to be stored separately to prevent a chemical reaction: the creation of water. With the addition of cornstarch to absorb the moisture, the chemicals could be stored together and were packaged as Rumsford Baking Powder. The invention of baking powder revolutionized baking, including biscuits. Baking powder negated the need for the laborious task of beating biscuits and produced a quick alternative to yeast bread. Recipes for baking powder biscuits have been found in most American cookbooks for the past 150 years. With the invention of baking powder, cooks could expect a high rise from biscuits. The flat biscuit gave rise to a preference for light, high, and fluffy biscuits.

Today, the modern American biscuit enjoys national popularity. Until recently, the biscuit wasn't given too much consideration outside of the southern United States. However, they've been a utility staple of Southern kitchens for more than four hundred years, used for sopping syrup and gravy, housing slices of ham, and as an ingredient in Southern dressings and stuffing. The recent popularity of biscuits in the Northeast has led to biscuit shops, some of which had to close down to retool and reorganize because they couldn't keep up with demand. All this attention has Southerners scratching their heads. We're not surprised that the rest of the country has fallen in love with biscuits; we simply wonder why it took four hundred years for that to happen.

Biscuits in My Kitchen—Products, Tips, Equipment

Products

When making biscuits, the type of flour matters. Light, flaky, and tender biscuits require the use of **soft winter wheat flour**. White Lily is the only brand of soft winter wheat flour I use, and it's the one I recommend. Soft winter wheat flour has less protein and less gluten than other types of flour. This results in dough that is more tender and flaky, both highly desirable qualities in modern biscuits. All my recipes have been tested with White Lily. I can't guarantee you'll get the same results from other brands or other types of flour. White Lily is the brand my grandmother used and it has been on the market since 1883.

Unsalted butter is preferred to salted butter. I ordinarily use self-rising flour, which has salt added. The butter must be cold and left in pieces the size of peas to get optimum flakiness from the dough. As the cold butter starts to melt in the dough while cooking, tiny air pockets form, which results in little layers of flakiness. There's not a particular brand I recommend, although I prefer organic from cows that haven't been fed antibiotics and hormones.

Buttermilk, and any dairy used in biscuits, should be very cold and full fat, although it's sometimes difficult to find full fat dairy products in grocery stores. If you can't find full fat, get the highest fat content available.

Tips

- Dip your biscuit cutter in flour to prevent it sticking to the dough. Always cut straight down and don't twist to get a better rise from the biscuits. It's harder for you to stand up straight when your underwear's twisted. The same holds true for biscuits.

- For a crunchier exterior, place biscuits apart on the baking sheet. For a softer exterior, place the biscuits touching. Biscuits that have been layered sometimes rise so high that it's easy for them to fall over. I always place those biscuits touching for more support.
- After cutting out the biscuits, gather the scraps, layer them, and gently pat them out to approximately the same thickness of the original dough. Layering and patting, instead of balling up the scraps, will make the second batch of cutouts just as pretty as the first.
- There is an art to biscuit making. First, have faith and pray for grace. Next, don't rely on a recipe to tell you the correct proportion of wet to dry ingredients. Make sure the dough is wet and sticky when you turn it out onto a floured surface. Sprinkle the wet dough with flour and gently work it into the dough, adding more as needed, until it's no longer sticky and it holds its shape. Rely on the dough and your hands to let you know when the dough is just right. The more you make biscuits, the better you will develop a feel for this. When following my recipes, you will always need more flour than called for in the recipe. The extra amount needed will vary depending on many factors, including types of ingredients used. A cup of buttermilk results in wetter dough than a cup of sour cream, for example. For that matter, different brands of buttermilk have different viscosity. For this reason, I don't indicate the amount of extra flour needed but, rather, give the instructions to continue adding flour and gently knead it in until the dough is no longer sticky and holds its shape.
- Cut, unbaked biscuits freeze well. Place them in a single layer on a waxed paper–lined baking sheet and freeze overnight. The next morning, transfer them to a sealable freezer bag (I use this method for freezing my blueberries, blackberries, and citrus slices). Take out the number of biscuits you need and bake in a preheated oven at the regular temperature for about five additional minutes or until tops are golden brown. If desired, brush tops with melted butter or cooking oil during last five minutes of bake time.

Equipment

You need a bowl big enough to move around in. A **large mixing bowl** will usually suffice if making one batch of biscuits at a time. I use a mixing bowl that I've had longer than I've had my husband. In fact, it was a wedding gift.

For cutting in the fat, you'll need either a **pastry cutter** or **forks**. I prefer to rub in the butter so no additional equipment is needed other than my fingers and thumb.

A **wooden spoon** is preferred to stainless steel for stirring in liquid because I think it's a little kinder to the dough.

Turning out the dough onto a **floured tea towel**, **nonstick mat**, or **waxed paper** makes clean up easier. Of the three, I prefer a tea towel.

I have a set of three **biscuit cutters** that are 2, 2½, and 3 inches. If you don't have biscuit cutters, you can use a small glass. In my neck of the woods, there's been a passel of biscuits cut out over the years with Vienna sausage cans and potted meat cans. (Biscuits don't have to be round. It's perfectly acceptable to cut out squares with a pizza cutter or sharp knife.)

For **baking sheets**, I prefer to cover them a **Silpat baking mat** instead of greasing them. I've never had a biscuit, or anything else, stick to one of those mats, which I've had for several years. They are a worthwhile investment.

Cast-iron skillets are the ideal cooking vessel for cat head biscuits. I use a cast-iron skillet for cut biscuits if I have a batch small enough to fit in one skillet. The size of baking sheets accommodates larger batches of cut biscuits better than skillets. My preferred brand for new cast-iron skillets is Lodge. I have several hand-me-down skillets and cast-iron pieces from unknown manufacturers. When I'm in the market for new pieces, I shop for Lodge exclusively. The skillets are high quality from a good American company.

Dough can either be rolled out with a **rolling pin** or patted out with your fingers. It's a personal preference and both methods are acceptable. If using a rolling pin, make certain the rolling and top of the dough is sufficiently floured to prevent sticking. Roll with a light touch.

Standard dry and liquid **measuring cups** and **measuring spoons** are also necessary. I measure dry ingredients instead of weighing them.

Biscuits in Grandmother's Kitchen

Biscuits are versatile and capable of being incorporated into all aspects of our food ways. This chapter contains basic biscuit recipes that make biscuits good enough to stand on their own or to be used as an ingredient in a more complicated recipe.

Biscuits can be categorized by the five techniques used to shape them. The ingredients for the dough vary. Once the dough is mixed, the instructions for shaping the biscuits are the same for each biscuit in the category. Listed below are the categories and the names of each biscuit included in this chapter.

The chapter on traditional biscuits likely to be products from your grandmother's kitchen wouldn't be complete without a recipe that my grandmother made for a dessert made from leftover biscuits.

Rolled or Patted, Layered, and Cut

The beautiful, tender, flaky layers coveted in today's biscuit are a result of three things: product, technique, and faith.

First, you must use the right products. Flour should be soft winter wheat flour which has a lower protein content than standard flour and keeps the dough tender and flaky. White Lily flour is my preferred brand. I prefer self-rising flour and can't understand, for the life of me, why some people treat self-rising flour as a product that's inferior to all-purpose. White Lily self-rising flour has just the right ratio of flour-to-leavening and never has an off-putting metallic taste. Butter should be very cold. Cube it and place it back in the refrigerator or use it immediately after cubing. Buttermilk, or other liquids, must be ice cold, also.

Next, a special layering technique builds layer upon layer much in the same way as puff pastry. An important part of technique is to handle the dough as little as possible. You want to get in and get out when you're making biscuits. Obviously, you must handle the dough. But biscuit-making time isn't when you want to lollygag around and make the process long and drawn out. Biscuits are quick breads. They're meant to be assembled and baked in short order.

Lastly, you need to keep the faith and pray for grace. Making biscuits isn't complicated but it does require "the touch." Turning out beautiful delicious biscuits is no different than varsity sports in that the more you practice, the better you become. You will develop the right feel for rubbing in the butter, knowing when the dough has enough flour and being able to develop the layers. Don't rely on a recipe for the correct ratio of wet-to-dry ingredients. I prefer to get my dough wet in the mixing bowl, turn it out onto a floured surface, and work in the right amount of additional flour until it's no longer sticky and it holds its shape. The amount of the last bit of flour needed will depend on several variables such as weather, viscosity of the liquid, and the type of flour used.

Instructions and Layering Technique

Add soft winter wheat flour and cubed, chilled unsalted butter in a large mixing bowl.

Rub in the butter by grabbing small amounts of the flour and butter between your thumb and fingers. Rub once and then release back into the bowl. Continue this process quickly all throughout the flour mixture. This is my preferred method. Alternatively, use a pastry cutter. Continue until the flour looks like coarse meal.

Pea-sized pieces of butter will remain.

Stir in buttermilk or other liquid with a wooden spoon. The dough will be wet and sticky.

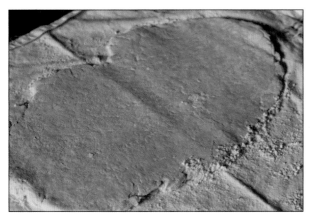

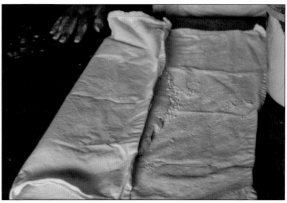

Turn the dough out onto a tea-towel that has been sprinkled with flour. Sprinkle the top of the wet dough with flour. Lightly knead the dough, working in the flour. Add more flour as needed until the dough is no longer sticky and holds its shape. Don't let a recipe dictate the proportions of wet to dry ingredients. Develop "the touch" and know when the dough feels right. Roll or pat out the dough until it's ¼-inch-thick long-ways on the towel. Make sure there is enough flour under the dough to prevent sticking.

Grab the right side of the towel and fold the right third of the dough toward the center.

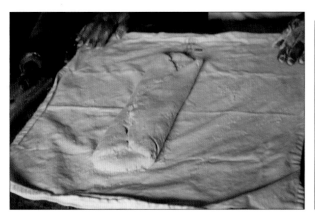

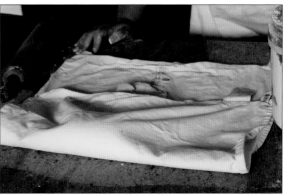

Grab the left side of the towel and fold the left third of the dough toward the center.

Grab the top of the towel and fold the dough in half from top to bottom.

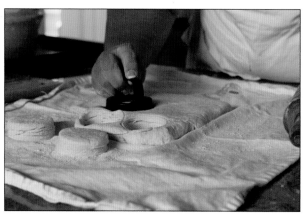

Grab the bottom of the towel and fold in dough in half bottom to top.

Lightly roll or pat out the dough to one-inch thick. Cut out the biscuits by using a floured biscuit cutter. Cut straight down and don't twist the biscuit cutter or the edges will bind together and prevent the biscuit from rising to its full potential. Just think about how hard it is to stand up straight and tall when your underwear is twisted.

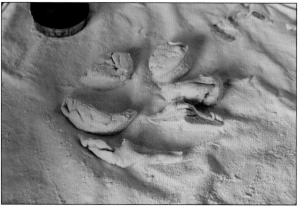

Continue cutting as many as biscuits as you can.

Gather the scraps, stack them, and gently press together. This method keeps the layers intact and will result in prettier biscuits than if you reroll the dough scraps. We all want pretty biscuits. The gently pressed layer of scraps needs to be about one-inch thick.

Cut as many biscuits as you can get.

This is what you're looking for: layers, glorious layers.

Place the cut out biscuits on a baking sheet that has been greased or covered with a baking mat. I find it best to scoot these layered biscuits next to each other to help them rise up straight and not fall over. Brush tops with cooking oil, butter, or milk.

Bake in a preheated 450-degree oven for 15 minutes or until tops are golden brown.

Apply these instructions for recipes on pages 29 to 39!
Angel Biscuits (35) and Gluten-free Biscuits (37) have their own set of instructions.

Buttermilk Biscuits

Yield: 12 to 15 (2½-inch) buttermilk biscuits

Preheat oven to 450°

This is my standard biscuit recipe. Buttermilk contains a mild acid that further tenderizes the already tender southern winter wheat flour. The flaky layers are the result of pea-sized pieces of butter left in the dough and a folding technique that builds layers similar to puff pastry. If you want to perfect one biscuit recipe for your favorite collection, this is it. Folks are fools for hot, flaky buttermilk biscuits.

2 cups soft winter wheat self-rising flour
½ cup unsalted butter, cubed and chilled
1 cup buttermilk

Baking Powder Biscuits

Yield: 12 to 15 biscuits

Preheat oven to 450°

The commercialization of baking powder dramatically changed the preparation technique of biscuits. Baking powder is a combination of baking soda, a mild acid such as cream of tartar, and a moisture-absorbing ingredient such as cornstarch. It's used as a leavening agent. Prior to the invention of baking powder in the nineteenth century, potash was used as leavening. The leavening capability of potash isn't nearly as potent as baking powder so the rise is less. Also, potash was homemade so it wasn't consistent in its composition. Commercially prepared baking powder was a trustworthy leavening agent that offered the same leavening action as yeast but acted immediately and didn't require the long rise times needed with yeast. Self-rising flour contains baking powder and all-purpose doesn't. Recipes for Baking Powder Biscuits are ubiquitous while basic biscuit recipes using self-rising flour aren't nearly as common. Perhaps the nostalgia of Baking Powder Biscuits has garnered fame yet to be shared by biscuits made with self-rising flour. Baking Powder Biscuits are historically significant. Self-rising flour arrived on the scene later but isn't an inferior product.

2 cups soft winter wheat all-purpose flour
1 tablespoon baking powder
1 teaspoon kosher salt
½ cup unsalted butter, diced and chilled
1 cup buttermilk

Place flour, baking powder, and salt in a large bowl and mix together with a fork or whisk.

Cornmeal Biscuits

Yield: 12 biscuits

Preheat oven to 450°

If biscuits and cornbread got married, their children would look a lot like cornmeal biscuits. The flakiness of a traditional buttermilk biscuit is there, but with an extra dose of texture from stone ground cornmeal. The small amount of cornmeal produces a surprisingly distinct corn flavor. I used all-purpose flour instead of self-rising because I wanted to have control over the amount of leavening and be sure to have enough to account for the addition of plain cornmeal. Serve these biscuits with a hearty stew.

1½ cups soft winter wheat all-purpose flour
2½ teaspoons baking powder
½ teaspoon kosher salt
½ cup cornmeal
½ cup unsalted butter, cubed and chilled
1 cup buttermilk

Stir together flour, baking powder, salt, and cornmeal.

Angel Biscuits

Yield: approximately 30 (2½-inch) biscuits

Preheat oven to 450°

Also known as Bride's Biscuits, these biscuits are so certain to be light and fluffy that even a new bride can't fail. The insurance policy comes in the form of yeast plus the leavening action of baking powder. When working with a large amount of flour, such as the amount in this recipe, I find it convenient to measure all the dry ingredients into a mixing bowl and then sift them into a large container, such as a stockpot, which will give ample room to work in the butter.

2 (¾-ounce) packages yeast
¼ cup warm tap water (110–115°)
$^1/_8$ teaspoon sugar
5 cups all-purpose flour
soft winter wheat
1 tablespoon baking powder

1 teaspoon baking soda
2½ tablespoons granulated sugar
1 teaspoon kosher salt
1 cup (2 sticks) unsalted butter, cubed and chilled
2 cups buttermilk

Dissolve sugar in warm water. Sprinkle yeast over top and gently swirl. Set aside. If the mixture bubbles, then the yeast is active. If it doesn't bubble, throw it out and start over.

Sift together flour, baking powder, baking soda, sugar, and salt.

Add cubed butter and rub it in with your fingers or cut it in with a pastry blender until the mixture resembles coarse meal.

Make a well in the center and pour in yeast and buttermilk. Stir until the dough is wet.

Cover with a kitchen towel and place in a warm spot for 1 hour.

After an hour, turn half the dough out onto a surface sprinkled with flour. Sprinkle enough flour on the top of the dough to keep it from being sticky.

Knead dough 6 or 7 times. Shape into a disk.

Roll out to ¾ inches thick. Dip 2½-inch biscuit cutter in flour. Cut biscuits and place 1 inch apart on a cookie sheet that been greased or covered with a baking mat.

Gather scraps and repeat until all the dough has been used.

Brush biscuits tops with cooking oil.

Bake in a 450° preheated oven for 12 to 15 minutes until tops are golden brown.

Gluten-Free Biscuits

Yield: 10 to 12 (2½ inch) biscuits.

Preheat oven to 450°

So many folks have wheat sensitivities in our society today. Using King Arthur Gluten-Free Multi-Purpose Flour, I was able to create a biscuit with a good flavor. The texture isn't as light and fluffy as biscuits made with soft wheat flour. The dough was crumbly and slightly harder to work with than my soft wheat biscuits. Nonetheless, this biscuit is a good substitution for those who avoid wheat. If using baking flour other than the one I used for testing, be sure to use a blend.

2 cups gluten–free multi–purpose flour mix
1 tablespoon baking powder
1 teaspoon kosher salt
½ cup unsalted butter, cubed and chilled
1 cup buttermilk

Add baking mix, baking powder, and salt to a bowl and stir with hands. Rub in butter until the flour looks like coarse cornmeal. Make a well and pour in buttermilk. Stir with a heavy spoon until dough is wet. Turn out onto a surface sprinkled with gluten-free flour. Sprinkle top of dough with flour. Knead gently, adding flour as needed, until dough is no longer sticky.

Roll out to a rectangle ¼-inch thick. Fold ⅓ of dough toward the center. Repeat with the other side. Fold dough in half from top to bottom. Roll out to a ¾-inch thickness. Cut with a 2½-inch biscuit cutter. Place on a prepared baking sheet one inch apart. Brush tops with cooking oil.

Bake for 12 to 15 minutes or until tops are brown.

Honey Whole Wheat Cream Biscuits

Yield: 15 (1½-inch) biscuits

Preheat oven to 450°

Honey and cream work together to soften the bold flavor of stone ground whole wheat flour. These biscuits are slightly denser than those made with only soft winter wheat. I just love the craggy appearance of these hearty biscuits. I feel like I need to wear a plaid flannel shirt while eating them. They have a personality and proudly display a marvelous flavor that can stand on its own with simply a pat of butter or a little more honey drizzled on if your sweet tooth is talking to you.

1½ cups stone ground whole wheat flour
½ cup all-purpose soft winter wheat flour
1 tablespoon baking powder
1½ teaspoons kosher salt
1 cup plus 4 tablespoons heavy cream
1 tablespoon honey

Stir together both flours, baking powder, and salt in a large mixing bowl.

Stir honey into cream and add to bowl.

Stir until dough is wet.

Rolled and Cut Biscuits

Rolled and cut biscuits are made similarly to rolled, layered, and cut. The difference is the dough is rolled or patted without layering. I typically use this method for dough with extra ingredients such as fruit, cheese, or herbs. Rolling or patting out the dough multiple times, as you do with the layering technique, can crush or mash the additional ingredients and the supplemental items add extra weight to the dough, which can make it more difficult to complete the folding technique. Tavern biscuits are historical and meant to be more like a cracker than a biscuit. Party biscuits should be a little on the flat side because they are folded in half after you cut them. An extra high rise would make them too large to bite without breaking into pieces. Because of the strong flavor of dill, I find a smaller biscuit more desirable. A little bit of dill goes a long way.

Sweet Potato Biscuits

Yield: about 24 (2½ inch) biscuits

Preheat oven to 450°

The goodness created when sweet potatoes marry homemade biscuits is the stuff about which movies are made. The flavors of sweet potato and spices bring personality to the biscuits without being overpowering. The biscuits are more like your favorite cousin and not like your least favorite great uncle.

3 cups soft winter wheat self-rising flour
¼ cup light brown sugar
½ teaspoon ground cinnamon
½ teaspoon ground ginger
¼ teaspoon ground nutmeg

½ cup unsalted butter, cubed and chilled
1 average-sized sweet potato, baked, cooled and peeled
1 cup half-and-half

Mix together flour, and next four ingredients. Cut in butter until flour mixture resembles coarse ground meal.

Add sweet potato. Mix with dry ingredients.

Pour in milk and mix, with spoon or hands, until incorporated. Dough will be wet and sticky.

Turn out dough onto a well-floured surface. Keep sprinkling flour on dough until it's no longer sticky and holds its shape. Roll out to 1-inch thick. Cut with 2½-in. biscuit cutter dipped in flour.

Place 1 inch apart on a sheet pan that has been sprayed with nonstick spray or covered with a baking mat. Brush tops with cooking oil or butter.

Bake in a 450° preheated oven for 12 to 15 minutes or until tops are golden brown.

Serve with Cinnamon Honey Butter.

Cinnamon Honey Butter

½ cup softened unsalted butter
1 tablespoon honey
½ teaspoon ground cinnamon

Garlic Cheese Biscuits

Yield: about 15 (2½ inch) biscuits

Preheat oven to 450°

The tang of extra-sharp cheddar cheese and aromatic punch of garlic combine to deliver a savory biscuit well suited to accompany almost any entrée.

2 cups self-rising soft winter wheat flour
¾ teaspoon garlic powder
½ teaspoon cayenne powder
1 cup shredded extra-sharp cheddar cheese
2 tablespoons fresh parsley, finely chopped
4 tablespoons unsalted butter, cubed and chilled
1 cup half-and-half

Mix flour, garlic powder, and cayenne pepper in a large bowl. Stir in cheese and parsley. Cut in butter until flour resembles coarse meal.

Make a well in the flour and pour in half-and-half. Stir until flour is wet and sticky. Turn out onto a generously floured surface. Sprinkle dough with enough flour to keep it from being sticky. Sprinkle flour on top and gently knead until dough is no longer sticky, adding flour as needed.

Roll out to 1-inch thick. Dip 2½-inch biscuit cutter into flour. Cut biscuits. Place 1 inch apart on a cookie sheet sprayed with nonstick spray or covered with a baking mat. Brush tops with cooking oil.

Bake at 450° in a preheated oven for 12 to 15 minutes or until tops are golden brown.

Tavern Biscuits

Yield: about 3 dozen (2½-inch) biscuits

Preheat oven to 400°

This recipe first appeared in Mary Randolph's The Virginia Housewife *in 1824. The dry ingredients were listed in weights and not measures with which American home cooks are familiar. I weighed the dry ingredients and converted to measures. Soft winter wheat flour is lighter than standard wheat flour. I substituted ground ginger for mace because I had ginger on hand and rarely use mace. I estimated "a glass of brandy" to be four ounces. This slightly sweet biscuit has a marvelous flavor and the appearance of a historical biscuit.*

3½ cups all-purpose soft winter wheat flour
1 cup granulated sugar
1 teaspoon ground nutmeg
½ teaspoon ground ginger

1 cup unsalted butter, cubed and chilled
½ cup brandy
½–¾ cup milk

Add flour, sugar, nutmeg, and ginger to a large mixing bowl and stir.

Rub or cut in butter until the flour resembles coarse meal. Stir in brandy.

Add milk until the dough is wet and forms a soft ball.

Turn out onto a well-floured surface. Roll out to rectangle ¼-inch thick. Cut with a 2 ½-inch biscuit cutter dipped in flour.

Gather scraps and repeat.

Place biscuits on a baking sheet that has been greased or covered in a baking mat.

Prick the tops of the biscuits a few times with the tines of a fork. Brush tops with cooking oil.

Bake for 17 minutes or until tops are golden brown. Check carefully during last few minutes of baking to make sure the bottoms are getting too brown. Remove them if the bottoms are browning too much.

> **TAVERN BISCUIT.**
>
> To one pound of flour, add half a pound of sugar, half a pound of butter, some mace and nutmeg powdered, and a glass of brandy or wine; wet it with milk, and when well kneaded, roll it thin, cut it in shapes, and bake it quickly.

Dill Buttermilk Biscuits

Yield: 12 (2½-inch) biscuits or 18 (2-inch) biscuits

Preheat oven to 450°

Dill can quickly overpower. It's not an herb that I want to use as the star of the show. Used in correct proportions, it can accentuate flavors nicely. Dill has an affinity for seafood, making dill biscuits a perfect choice to serve alongside, or as a part of, any seafood dish. If these biscuits are to be used as a bread accompaniment for a seafood dish, I recommend cutting them to a smaller size. A small bite goes a long way.

2 cups self-rising soft winter wheat flour
½ cup unsalted butter, cubed and chilled
2 tablespoons fresh dill, finely minced
1 cup buttermilk

Add flour and butter to a large bowl. Cut or rub in butter until it resembles coarse meal. Stir in fresh dill.

Add buttermilk and stir with a wooden spoon until the flour is wet.

Turn out dough onto a well-floured surface. Sprinkle flour over dough, gently knead and work it in, adding more as needed, until the dough is no longer sticky and holds its shape.

Roll or pat out dough to 1-inch thick.

Cut with biscuit cutter dipped in flour.

Place on baking sheet that has been sprayed with nonstick spray or covered with a baking mat.

Brush tops with cooking oil.

Bake in a 450° preheated oven for 12 to 15 minutes or until the tops are golden brown.

Mashed Potato Biscuits

Yield: 12 to 14 (2½-inch biscuits)

Preheat oven to 450°

Leftover mashed potatoes at my house were usually mixed with an egg, flour, and a little bit of onion, shaped into a patty, and fried. We called these potato fritters. I found adding some leftover mashed potatoes to biscuit dough gives the biscuit a nice soft texture.

2 cups soft winter wheat self–rising flour
½ cup unsalted butter, cubed and chilled
½ cup leftover mashed potatoes
1 cup buttermilk

Add flour to a large bowl. Cut or rub in butter until flour resembles coarse meal.

Stir in mashed potatoes and buttermilk until the flour is wet. Turn dough out onto a well-floured surface. Sprinkle the tops of the dough with flour. Gently knead and work in the flour, adding more as needed, until the dough is no longer sticky and holds its shape.

Party Biscuits

Yield: about 30 (2-inch) biscuits

Preheat oven to 450°

*Henrietta Dull shared a recipe for what she called Party Biscuits in her 1928 cookbook, **Southern Cooking**. Her recipe calls for an egg and a little bit of sugar, which I omitted and then followed my standard buttermilk biscuit recipe. I did incorporate her technique for folding the cut-out biscuit in half like a Parker House roll. You'll need to cook in batches.*

2 cups soft winter wheat self-rising flour
½ cup unsalted butter, cubed and chilled
1 cup buttermilk
Additional melted butter

Add flour to a large mixing bowl. Rub or cut in butter until flour resembles coarse meal. Stir in buttermilk with a wooden spoon until dough is wet. Turn out dough onto a well-floured surface. Sprinkle flour on top of dough. Gently knead the dough and work in the flour, adding more as needed, until dough is no longer sticky and holds its shape.

Roll out to rectangle ¼-inch thick. Cut out with a 2-inch biscuit cutter dipped in flour.

Place biscuits on a baking sheet that has been greased or covered with a baking mat.

Brush top of biscuit with melted butter. Fold in half with melted butter on the inside of the biscuit.

Bake in a 450° oven for 12 minutes or until golden brown.

Repeat with remaining dough.

Drop Biscuits

Drop biscuits save time by taking away the step of rolling and cutting biscuits. The biscuit dough is mixed and dropped onto a baking sheet while the dough is still sticky and wet. Instead of dropping dough from a spoon, I use an ice cream scoop so the dough maintains more of rounded, uniform shape.

Cream Biscuits

Yield: about 12 to 13 biscuits

Preheat oven to 450°

Cream biscuits are a sweet little biscuit in every way possible. They are easy to make, taste slightly sweet, and are as tender and fluffy as clouds. The substantial fat content of heavy cream is sufficient and eliminates the step of cutting in cubes of butter or shortening. The sweet overtone makes them an ideal dessert biscuit, a perfect partner for salty country ham, or an afternoon teatime treat. This recipe is a good starting point for novice biscuit bakers.

2 cups soft winter wheat self-rising flour
1 tablespoon granulated sugar
1½ cups heavy cream

Mix flour and sugar in a large mixing bowl. Pour in cream and stir until flour is wet. Scoop out the dough with a greased ⅓ cup ice cream scoop.

Place 2 inches apart on a baking sheet well-greased or covered with a baking mat.

Bake in a preheated 450° oven for 12 to 15 minutes or until golden brown.

Sour Cream and Chive Drop Biscuits

Yield: 12 to 13 biscuits

Preheat oven to 450°

Sour cream adds tang and moisture to the dough and chives add a desirable, herby, savory flavor that makes these biscuits a fine dinner bread.

2 cups soft winter wheat self-rising flour
1 tablespoon sugar
½ cup unsalted butter, diced and chilled

3 tablespoons chives, chopped
8 ounces sour cream
1 cup buttermilk

Place flour and sugar in a bowl. Cut or rub in butter until flour resembles coarse meal. Add remaining ingredients and stir until mixed.

Using a ⅓ cup ice cream scoop, drop even amounts of dough onto a baking sheet oiled or covered with a baking mat.

Bake in a 450° preheated oven for 15 to 18 minutes or until tops are golden brown.

Free Hand

Pieces of dough are pinched off and patted by hand to form a rustic biscuit with a free-form shape. No two biscuits will be exactly the same, which adds to the charm.

These biscuits come together quicker than rolled-and-cut biscuits. The dough stays in the bowl and doesn't have to be turned out onto a floured surface. Theoretically, this makes clean up easier. I seem to find ways to scatter flour all over tarnation regardless of the biscuit making method.

Cathead 59
Bacon Cathead 61

Cathead Biscuits

Preheat oven to 450°

Cathead biscuits ain't no dainty biscuit. They're big, craggy, and rustic; sort of like a backwoodsman. Serve these for a hardy breakfast or with a meaty stew, but select a more appropriate biscuit, such as cream biscuits, for afternoon tea. Cathead biscuits would not know how to dress or act appropriately at teatime. Considering the rough texture and similar personality of these biscuits, brush the tops with bacon drippings instead of a more delicate fat like cooking oil or butter.

1 generous tablespoon (very generous) bacon drippings

2 cups soft winter wheat self-rising flour

½ cup unsalted butter, cubed and chilled

1 cup buttermilk

Melt the bacon drippings in a 10-inch cast-iron skillet. Pour excess into a cup and set aside. Leave residual drippings in the skillet.

Place flour in a large bowl. Cut in butter until the flour resembles coarse meal.

Pour in buttermilk and stir until you have a wet and sticky dough.

Turn out dough onto a floured surface. Sprinkle top with flour until dough is no longer sticky.

Knead 4 or 5 times, adding flour as needed, until dough isn't sticky and holds its shape. Form into a disc and divide into 8 equal portions using your hands. To maintain the authentic uneven surface, don't roll with a rolling pin or cut with a biscuit cutter.

Gently shape each piece of dough into a round by rolling between your hands. Place in the skillet that was used to melt bacon drippings. One biscuit goes in the center with 7 surrounding it. Mash the biscuit dough down with the back of your fingers until all the biscuits are touching. You should be able to see ridges in the dough.

Brush the tops with reserved bacon drippings.

Bake in a 450° preheated oven for 15 minutes or until tops are golden brown. Serve directly from the skillet.

Bacon Cathead Biscuits

Yield: 8 biscuits

Preheat oven to 450°

You can put slices of bacon on your biscuit and create something wonderful. However, working bacon into your biscuit dough is biscuit bliss. The craggy, rustic, and rugged nature of cathead biscuits and the commonness of smoky bacon is the perfect marriage. If you infuse bacon bits into the biscuit dough, it's only right that you brush the tops with bacon drippings.

4 slices bacon, cooked until crispy★
2 cups soft winter wheat self-rising flour
4 tablespoons unsalted butter, cubed and chilled
1 cup buttermilk

★ Reserve 2 tablespoons of drippings to brush the tops of the biscuits.

Add flour to bowl and cut or rub in butter until flour resembles coarse meal. Stir in diced bacon.

Form a well in flour and pour in buttermilk. Stir with a wooden spoon until dough is wet.

If dough is too sticky to handle, sprinkle flour on top and work in until it's no longer sticky. Separate the dough in 8 equal portions and roll each into a ball with your hands.

Place the dough pieces into a 9- or 10-inch cast-iron skillet coated with bacon drippings. I use the skillet in which I cooked the bacon. Press down the dough with the back of your fingers until the dough covers the bottom of the skillet. Brush tops with reserved bacon drippings.

Bake in a 450° preheated oven 15 minutes or until the tops are golden brown.

Loaf

Baking biscuit dough into a loaf shortens the work time and shows the versatility and forgiveness of the dough. Prior to testing this recipe, I was interested to see if the middle of the loaf cooked completely before the outside burned. It worked well and produced a nice loaf of biscuit bread.

Biscuit dough conforms well to a loaf shape. For best results, let the loaf cool completely before cutting.

Yogurt Biscuit Bread 62
Rosemary Focaccia Biscuit Bread 65

Yogurt Biscuit Bread

Yield: 4 (4-inch) squares

Preheat oven to 450°

Sourdough bread is made from using a centuries' old technique of fermenting yeast cultures, which gives the dough its characteristic sour flour. Plain yogurt mixed with flour produces the same sour-flavored batter. Sourdough bread requires a starter which takes time to make. Yogurt Biscuit Bread only requires self-rising flour and yogurt and is ready to make when you're ready. As with all yeast breads, the texture is different than that of quick breads such as biscuits. I find the flavor of this biscuit bread outstanding and it improves the second day. To get more of a bread experience, I baked the bread into a loaf instead of individual biscuits. Nathalie Dupree includes a recipe called Busty Yogurt Biscuits in **Southern Biscuits** *and she discusses the varying consistencies of yogurt. I used twice as much yogurt as Nathalie's recipe, which shows the wide variation in the amount of yogurt needed to get the dough to the desired consistency. The ingredients need to be incorporated and the dough must be workable.*

2 cups soft winter wheat self-rising flour   16 ounces plain yogurt
4 tablespoons unsalted butter, cubed and chilled

Rub butter into flour until it resembles coarse meal. Stir in yogurt until the flour and yogurt are mixed.

Cover the bottom and insides of an 8x8-inch pan with parchment paper. Spoon batter onto paper and spread evenly. Lightly brush top with oil.

Bake for 20 minutes or until top is brown and toothpick inserted comes out clean.

Rosemary Focaccia Biscuit Bread

Yield: 4 (4 inch) squares

Preheat oven to 450°

Focaccia bread is that wonderful bread served in Italian restaurants for dipping in olive oil. I researched lots of focaccia bread recipes to determine the main characteristics that would help me develop a focaccia-style biscuit bread. Olive oil, herbs, and garlic are commonly used for flavor. The characteristically craggy appearance on the top is made by forming indentions with your knuckles.

2½ cups soft winter wheat self-rising flour
1 tablespoon finely minced fresh rosemary
½ teaspoon garlic powder
1 cup buttermilk
½ cup olive oil
1 tablespoon grated Parmesan cheese

Place flour in a large bowl. Stir in rosemary and garlic powder.

Add milk and olive oil. Stir until dough is wet.

Cover the inside of 8x8-inch baking dish with parchment paper. Sprinkle dough with olive oil and spread dough evenly over paper.

Make indentations over the entire top surface of the dough with your knuckles. Sprinkle with Parmesan cheese.

Bake in a 450° preheated oven for 15 minutes or until top is brown and inside of bread is done.

Remove and let cool on cooling rack.

A collection of vintage enamelware used by my grandmother to make cobblers and biscuit pudding.

Leftovers: Be Smart

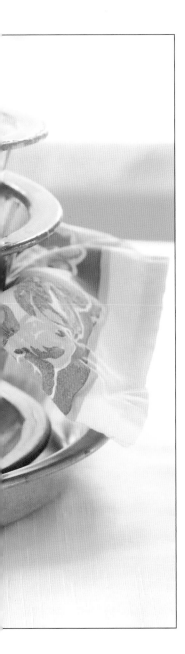

In my grandmother's eyes, throwing away food was a sin against God and all creation. She frequently gave me lessons on how to "be smart" and use up leftovers, as well as how to create meals from things you had on hand, which she called "making good with what you've got." Those lessons of thriftiness and frugality extended beyond the kitchen. She and my granddaddy had the innate gift of being able to find ingenious ways to reuse things, as did so many folks of their generation. Today, we are a disposable society and many of the smart ideas to reuse products have been lost. We throw away tons of food, too.

She taught me how to use leftover biscuits to make a pudding. Her method fell right in line with her frugal way of thinking.

"Don't mess up any more dishes than's called for. You can mix all the fixin's right in the dish you're a-gonna bake in," she advised.

She cooked by sight, not by book. Her instructions were usually vague and incomplete.

"Crumble you up some leftover biscuits in a pan. Then, pour over enough good milk to cover them. They need to set (sit) for long enough that they can get good 'n' soft. Then sprinkle a good cupful of sugar over them and stir it with your fork. Now, you need to add you in some eggs to make the pudding set up real good. Whip 'em in with your fork as you go. If you've got some vaniller flavoring, add you in some of that. Last thing to do is to chip you up some butter over the top. Put it in a oven that's not as hot as you need to bake biscuits 'cause the biscuits is already done. Take it out when it's done."

I've deciphered and decoded Granny's instructions to meet our modern-day expectations of explicit recipe directions. However, I hope the old-timey notions of "be smart" and "make good with what you've got" stay with me. For more recipes using leftover biscuits, see Cornish Games Hens with Cornmeal Biscuit Dressing, page 147, and Skillet Toasted Biscuits with Herb Cream Cheese and Country Tomato Relish, page 140.

Raspberry Biscuit Pudding
with Vanilla Ice Cream Sauce

Yield: 6 to 8 servings

Preheat oven to 350°

Buttermilk biscuits work best for this, although, a sweet biscuit would be good, too, with the amount of sugar in the pudding adjusted. The addition of raspberries was my idea. If my grandmother ever added fresh fruit to her biscuit pudding, I don't remember it. Crumble the biscuits in chunks. You don't want to start with biscuit crumbs.

4 cups leftover biscuits, gently crumbled
2 cups half-and-half or milk
1 cup granulated sugar
4 eggs, beaten
1 teaspoon vanilla extract

½ teaspoon ground cinnamon
12 ounces fresh raspberries
4 tablespoons of unsalted butter, cubed
1 cup premium vanilla ice cream, melted

Grease an 8x8-inch baking dish. Add crumbled biscuits.

Pour half-and-half over biscuits and let sit for 10 to 15 minutes until the biscuits are soft.

Sprinkle sugar over top and mix in with a fork.

Pour in beaten eggs, vanilla extract, and cinnamon and mix into bread mixture with a fork, making sure all ingredients are well incorporated.

Sprinkle raspberries on top and gently press down.

Sprinkle cubed butter over top.

Bake in a preheated 350° oven for 45 minutes. When done, the center will jiggle but it shouldn't slosh.

Let cool 15 minutes before serving. The center may have risen during baking, but it will collapse when cooled.

Drizzle with vanilla sauce before serving. If you prefer to omit vanilla ice cream sauce, sprinkle a little bit of sugar over the berries before baking.

Vanilla Sauce

Melt 1 cup premium vanilla ice cream.

Biscuits in Bakery Shops

The good Lord knows that we Southerners love our sweets. We're famous for grand layer cakes such as Red Velvet, Coconut, Lane, Hummingbird, Blackberry Jam, 1-2-3-4, Italian Cream, Carrot, and Caramel. We make endless varieties of Pound Cake, any kind of cobbler and pie imaginable, and sheet cakes to beat the band. Our cookie jars are always filled and we make candy at Christmas like it's going to be the last Christmas. To say we have an affinity for sugar is like saying fish prefer to stay a little damp. When it comes to sugar, we just can't help ourselves. It's only right that a cookbook about biscuits contain a chapter on dessert.

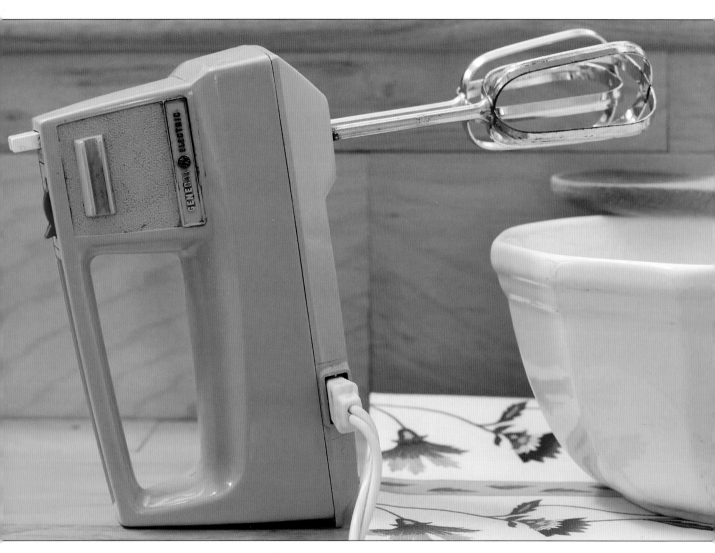

My hand mixer is forty years old. It keeps on ticking.

Strawberry Fields

Strawberry Shortcake was always a favorite childhood dessert. Neither the shortcake nor the whipped cream was ever homemade. My mother and grandmother opted for store-bought pound cake or the little sponge cake cups, the latter of which we all thought was a spectacular and amazing product. A can of Reddi-Whip was ready when we needed it for the whipped cream topping.

The process leading up to strawberry shortcake added to the special nature of the dessert. The best container of strawberries was handpicked from the sea of containers in the grocery store produce section. The strawberries were washed, hulled, and sliced into a large bowl. A discussion would ensue regarding the right quantity of sugar needed to "sugar them down." The strawberries were sugared, stirred, and placed in the refrigerator. They were checked and stirred frequently to determine if the sugar had melted and berries had released enough juice to make a sufficient amount of syrup. Finally, we were dished out plates of strawberry shortcake with just the right amount of juice, but never enough whipped topping. Those cans of Reddi-Whip don't hold much and there was always fear we'd run out. So, the whipped topping was doled out scantily, which never made sense to me because the can was always found the next day in the door of the refrigerator and it still had whipped topping in it.

Because of this special dessert, I dreamed of walking in a strawberry field and plucking strawberries from the plant. I imagined a strawberry field at the peak of the season must be the most beautiful sight in the world. Apparently, I sealed my fate with those recurring dreams. My husband and I moved to the Tampa, Florida, suburbs in 1985, which happens to be the Winter Strawberry Capital of the World. Roadside strawberry stands serve up all sorts of strawberry desserts during the harvest season. Our favorite spot has tables and chairs set up outside next to the strawberry fields. Not only do you get a spectacular strawberry dessert, like strawberry shortcake, but you sit outside and overlook the beautiful strawberry fields bursting with gorgeous red jewels. A visit to the strawberry shortcake stand is truly one of life's simple pleasures.

I make Strawberry Shortcake quite a bit and enjoy trying out different recipes for shortcake. Sweet biscuits are the best for flavor and texture. They hold up to the strawberry syrup better than pound cake and have just the right of sweetness. I almost always make fresh whipped cream. It's so easy and doesn't take more than a couple of minutes. Plus, I love to pull out my forty-year-old General Electric hand mixer to make the whipped cream. I've had the mixer, a wedding shower gift, longer than I've had my husband. Imagine buying a mixer now and expecting to have it in working condition in the year 2054.

Double-decker Strawberry Shortcake

Yield: 12 servings

Preheat oven to 400°

I use cream cheese to make the cake sturdy and able to hold up to thick layers of whipped cream and straw-berries. In addition to the leavening in the flour, the dough gets an added boost from a carbonated beverage. Unlike traditional shortcake, which adds the strawberries and syrup directly on top of the shortcake and can't be assembled until serving time, this shortcake may be assembled ahead of time. The whipped cream adds a layer of protection to the cake and keeps it from absorbing too much liquid. For best results, spoon on the berries with a slotted spoon and save the reserved syrup to drizzle over the shortcake just prior to serving. Because the whipped cream is a barrier, the extra syrup would simply run down the sides of the shortcake and puddle under it.

Strawberry topping:

5 cups fresh strawberries, hulled and sliced—approximately 1½ (16 ounces) containers
½ cup sugar

Biscuit shortcake:

2 cups winter wheat self-rising flour
2 tablespoons sugar
½ cup unsalted butter, cubed and chilled

4 ounces full fat cream cheese, cubed
½–¾ cup lemon-lime flavored carbonated beverage
1 tablespoon unsalted butter, melted

Whipped cream:

16 ounces heavy whipping cream
¼ to ½ cup granulated sugar, depending on your
    taste preference

1 teaspoon vanilla extract

For strawberry topping:

Stir strawberries and sugar together in a large bowl. Place in refrigerator until sugar has dissolved and formed syrup.

For biscuit shortcake:

Add flour and sugar to a large mixing bowl and stir.

Rub or cut in butter until all the butter has been coated in flour. Large chunks may remain.

Rub or cut in cream cheese until all the cream cheese has been coated with butter and all the flour has been incorporated.

Stir in enough carbonated beverage until the dough is wet.

Turn out onto a well-floured surface. Sprinkle top of dough with flour. Gently knead, working in the flour and adding more as necessary until the dough is no longer sticky and holds its shape.

Divide the dough in half. Gently roll out the dough until it's the approximate dimensions of your baking dish. Grease the dish well. I used a 10x7 dish but 8x8 or 9x9 would work, too.

Place the dough in the baking dish and pat it out to cover the bottom. Brush top of dough with melted butter.

Roll out second half of dough to the approximate dimensions of the baking dish. Gently press the dough to fit over the dough in the baking dish.

Lightly brush the top with melted butter, if desired. I used the butter left on the pastry brush and in the cup where I melted the butter.

Bake at 400° for 20 minutes or until the top is golden brown. Remove from the oven and let cool in pan for 10 minutes. Then, remove to a cooling rack and let cool completely before attempting to separate the layers.

For whipped cream:

Combine all ingredients and beat with an electric mixer until stiff peaks form. Don't overbeat or you'll wind up with sweetened vanilla butter.

To assemble:

Place 1 layer of shortcake on a serving platter. Spread half the whipped cream. Spoon half the berries with a slotted spoon onto the whipped cream. Top with remaining layer of shortcake. Spread the remaining whipped cream over the shortcake. Spoon on remaining berries with a slotted spoon. Reserve syrup to drizzle over the individual servings of shortcake just before serving.

Full fat whipped cream will keep the shortcake from getting soggy. However, reserving the extra syrup is better than pouring it all on top of the whipped cream because it will only run down the sides and puddle under the cake.

Double-decker Strawberry Shortcake

Maple Cinnamon Rolls
with Buttermilk Maple Icing

Yield: 12 rolls

Preheat oven to 450°

Our church hosted a dinner in conjunction with a dessert auction to raise money for our mission projects. When asked to contribute a dessert for the auction, I said yes. I don't have the skills to decorate an elaborate dessert and create a work of art. However, I can bake something tasty and visually appealing. Our friends, Parker and Shari Keen, bid on and won the cinnamon rolls. The name of the baker/contributor for each dessert wasn't disclosed. Upon winning, Shari contacted me immediately to tell me they won cinnamon rolls that looked like mine. She asked me to confirm their eager anticipation that I had, indeed, made the cinnamon rolls. I was happy to be able to contribute to our fundraising efforts and equally happy to share a goody from my kitchen with cherished friends.

Dough:

1 batch of buttermilk biscuit dough (see page 29)
Roll out dough to a rectangle ¼ inch thick.

Icing:

2 cups powdered sugar
2 tablespoons melted butter
2 tablespoons grade B maple syrup
1 teaspoon vanilla extract
4 tablespoons buttermilk

Stir all ingredients together and whisk until smooth.

Filling:

2 sticks (1 cup) unsalted butter, softened
2 tablespoons grade B maple syrup
2 teaspoons cinnamon

Whip all ingredients together using an electric mixer until light and fluffy.

RECIPE FOR **Maple Cinnamon**

Rolls with Buttermilk Maple Icing

PREPARATION TIME _____ SERVINGS _____

To assemble:

Spread filling evenly on dough rectangle. Make sure to get as close to the edge of the dough as possible.

Starting with the edge of the dough farthest away from you, roll up in jellyroll fashion and form a log. When complete, pinch the seams together. Even out the thickness of the log by running your hands up and down the length.

Divide dough into 12 equal pieces. Place on a greased baking sheet or divide between 2 (8-inch) round pans that have been greased.

Bake in a preheated 450° oven for 18 minutes or until tops are brown.

Remove from oven. Pour icing over rolls while they are still in the pan and warm.

Let cool slightly and serve.

Chocolate Toffee Monkey Bread

Yield: 1 (9-inch) round loaf

Preheat oven to 350°

Monkey Bread is a familiar kid-friendly dessert that I remember making in Girl Scouts. I gussied it up a bit by adding toffee bits to the bread and a generous helping of chocolate glaze.

4 (7.5-ounce) cans buttermilk biscuits, divided
¾ cup granulated sugar
2½ teaspoons ground cinnamon
1 cup toffee bits, divided

½ cup butter
¾ cup brown sugar, packed
12 ounces semi-sweet chocolate chips

Cut 2 cans of biscuits into fourths.

Place granulated sugar and cinnamon into gallon-sized disposable bag. Shake to mix. In batches, add quartered biscuits to sugar mixture, shake well to coat, and place them in a tube pan that has been sprayed with non-stick spray.

After 2 cans of sugared biscuits quarters have been layered in a tube pan, sprinkle on ½ cup of toffee bits.

Repeat with remaining biscuits and toffee bits.

Put butter and brown sugar in a small saucepan. Heat until butter is melted and mixture is pourable. Pour over top of biscuits and toffee bits in tube pan.

Bake in a 350° preheated oven for 45 minutes or until biscuits are brown. Remove from oven. Let sit in tube pan for 5 minutes. Invert onto a plate.

Melt chocolate chips in the microwave for 90 seconds. Stir. Heat for 30 seconds and stir. Continue heating and stirring in 30 second increments until the chips are about 75 percent melted. Then, stir until completely melted. Drizzle over monkey bread.

Makin' Doughnuts

I was quite young when my grandmother introduced me to canned biscuits doughnuts. She made the hole with her thumb initially. When two-liter soft drinks came on the market, she delighted in teaching me that the bottle cap made the perfect-sized hole and the somewhat jagged edge helped to cut through the dough. Her excitement at this discovery was sweet and innocence like a child. Coca-Cola can never appreciate the joy they bestowed upon a simple, down-home country woman who discovered a clever use for a bottle cap. I can never thank Coca-Cola enough for the memory.

Granny's secret to the success of her biscuit doughnuts, in her estimation, is to use "the least little doughnuts you can find." I strayed from her training and tried using jumbo biscuits, thinking big doughnuts would be better than little doughnuts. That little experiment taught me, once again, that Granny was right. Jumbo biscuits browned too much on the outside before the insides finished. Granny was always right.

Biscuit Doughnuts

Yield: 20 doughnuts and 20 holes

Heat oil to 350°

Fresh hot doughnuts fry up quick and easy. Get kids in the kitchen with you when you make these. They love to cut out the holes and roll the doughnuts in sugar or dip them in glaze. Don't get distracted while they're frying or you will be disappointed to find you've got burned biscuits.

Doughnuts:

2 (7.5-ounce) cans buttermilk biscuits
Cooking oil

Remove biscuits from package. Using an object that's about 1 inch in diameter, such as a bottle top, cut a hole from the center of each biscuit.

Place enough cooking oil in a heavy pot or skillet that it comes up 1 to 2 inches on the side. Heat to 350°.

Fry doughnuts and holes in batches, careful not to crowd. In my 10-inch cast-iron pan, I fry 4 biscuits and 4 holes at once.

Fry for 30 to 45 seconds on one side until golden brown. Flip and do the same with the other side. Remove and drain on a brown paper sack.

As soon as they are cool enough to handle, dip in glaze or cover in cinnamon sugar.

Serve warm.

Orange Buttermilk Glaze

2 cups powdered sugar
3 tablespoons buttermilk

1 teaspoon orange extract
½ teaspoon vanilla extract

Whisk together all ingredients.

Cinnamon Sugar

½ cup granulated sugar

1 teaspoon ground cinnamon

Place both ingredients in a quart-sized plastic bag. Shake to mix.

Chocolate Chip Biscuits

Award-Winner!

with Strawberry Cream Cheese Filling

Yield: 16

Preheat oven to 450°

Chocolate and strawberry is a winning flavor combination and doesn't disappoint in the jelly roll style dessert. I surprised the ladies in my Bible study class with a batch of these and one of them remarked, "These are the best biscuits I've ever eaten in my life." Not only are these good biscuits, they're award-winning biscuits. This little biscuit won second place in the International Biscuit Festival 2014.

Filling:

8 ounces cream cheese, softened
½ cup strawberry jam

Biscuits:

2 cups soft winter wheat self-rising flour
½ cup unsalted butter, cubed and chilled
1 cup milk chocolate chips
1 cup buttermilk

For filling:

Mix with an electric mixer until smooth. Set aside

For biscuits:

Place flour in bowl and rub in butter until flour resembles coarse meal. Add in chocolate chips.

Stir in buttermilk until dough is sticky.

Turn out dough onto a floured surface. Sprinkle flour on dough and work it in the dough until it's no longer sticky. Form a ball from the dough.

Roll out to ½ inch thick.

Spread filling over dough. You might have a little filling left over.

Starting with the long edge farthest away, loosely roll toward you in jelly roll fashion, finishing with seam down. Even out the thickness of the dough by rubbing your hands up and down the roll.

Cut crosswise into 16 equal pieces. Place on a large baking sheet sprayed with non-stick spray or covered with a baking mat.

Bake in a 450° preheated oven for 15 minutes or until biscuits are lightly brown.

Remove from oven. Cool completely and drizzle with chocolate glaze.

Chocolate Glaze

1 cup milk chocolate chips   1 tablespoon half-and-half

Place chocolate chips and half-and-half in the top of a double boiler. Stir occasionally. When chips are about 75 percent melted, remove from heat and stir until completely melted. Drizzle over biscuits.

Strawberries and Cream Biscuits

Yield: 12 to 15 biscuits

Preheat oven to 450°

Baking fresh strawberries into dough can be tricky. They give off a lot of water and can easily make the dough gummy and seemingly undercooked, resulting in an undesirable texture. My friend, Shari, was with me in the kitchen the day I made these. She was happy to take on the job of Chief Quality Control Inspector. The biscuits passed Shari's approval and she gave the texture high marks.

2 cups soft winter wheat self-rising four
1 tablespoon sugar
½ cup unsalted butter
1 cup fresh strawberries, diced
1 cup plus 1 tablespoon heavy cream
Cooking oil and granulated sugar for tops

Place flour and sugar in a large bowl. Cut or rub in butter until flour resembles coarse meal.

Add strawberries and heavy cream. Stir until dough is wet and sticky.

Turn out onto a well-floured surface. Sprinkle dough with flour and gently knead, adding additional flour as needed until dough is no longer sticky.

Roll out to 1 inch thick. Cut with a 2½-inch biscuit cutter dipped in flour. Place on a baking sheet oiled or covered in a baking mat.

Brush tops of biscuits with cooking oil. Sprinkle with granulated sugar.

Bake in a preheated 450° oven for 15 minutes or until tops are golden brown.

Strawberry Banana Nut Biscuit Bread

with Buttermilk Orange Glaze

Yield: one loaf

Preheat oven to 350°

I participate in a fun social media group that's all about food. It's spearheaded by the food editor of one of our local newspapers. Using Twitter as our platform, we gather once a week to discuss a preselected food topic. Additionally, we're presented a recipe and challenged to cook it, photograph it, and comment on it. You're encouraged to be as creative as you'd like or follow the recipe closely. It's your choice. One of the challenge recipes was Strawberry Bread with Honey Butter. After adding my twists and turns to the recipe, I wound up with a slightly different version. Using my standard biscuit recipe, I substituted sour cream for buttermilk, added baking soda to the sour cream for more lift, and put in a little sugar, flavorings, nuts, strawberries, and bananas. Instead of honey butter for a smear, I made a buttermilk orange glaze.

½ cup unsalted butter, softened
¾ cup granulated sugar
8 ounces sour cream
1 teaspoon baking soda
1 cup diced strawberries

½ medium banana, diced
1 cup chopped pecans
½ teaspoon vanilla extract
½ teaspoon orange extract
2 cups soft winter wheat self–rising flour

Using an electric mixer, cream together butter and sugar until light in texture and pale yellow in appearance. Add vanilla and orange extracts and mix.

Stir together sour cream and baking soda in a bowl. Set aside. If the mixture expands, you will know that your baking soda is active. If it doesn't expand, discard your baking soda and make a trip to the store.

Mix together strawberries, banana, and pecans. Set aside.

Add a small amount, about ⅓ or less of the flour to the creamed butter mixture in the mixing bowl. Pulse until flour is mixed in. Mix in half the sour cream mixture. Continue alternating until flour and sour cream are mixed into the dough.

Gently fold in fruits and nuts.

Spread dough evenly in a 9x5-inch loaf pan prepared with a nonstick baking spray.

Bake in a 350° preheated oven for 60 minutes or until toothpick inserted comes out clean. Cool in pan on a wire rack for 30 minutes.

Buttermilk Orange Glaze

1 cup powdered sugar
2 tablespoons buttermilk
1 teaspoon orange extract

Mix together with spoon until smooth. Drizzle over bread as soon as it's taken out of the loaf pan.

King Cake

Yield: one cake

Preheat oven to 350°

King Cake is more like a pastry than a cake. It's a tradition tied to Mardi Gras that dates back to early Christianity. The colors of the icing are the colors of Mardi Gras, and each have significance: purple for justice, green for faith, and gold for power. Baby Jesus, the King, is hidden in the cake. Tradition holds that the one who finds the baby Jesus will have good luck throughout the year. Frozen bread dough can be used for a shortcut. Following the spiritual theme of King Cake, I thought there was only one logical choice for a biscuit dough: angel biscuits.

Dough:

One batch of Angel Biscuit dough

Filling:

8 ounces cream cheese, softened
1 cup powdered sugar

Zest of one lemon
Juice of ½ lemon

Prepare angel biscuit dough (see page 35). Place in a well-greased bowl and let rise for one hour in a warm place free from drafts. After one hour, turn dough out onto a well-floured surface. Sprinkle with flour and gently knead, adding flour as needed, until dough is no longer sticky.

Roll out dough to a rectangle ½-inch thick.

Prepare filling by mixing all ingredients with an electric mixer until smooth. Spread evenly over dough.

Starting at the long edge, roll dough toward center and form a log. Pinch seams together and form a circle or oval with the log. Move to a baking sheet been sprayed with a nonstick spray or covered with a baking mat. Let rise in a warm draft-free area for 1 hour.

Bake in a 350° oven for 30 minutes or until golden brown.

Let cool before icing.

Insert baby Jesus into the loaf in an inconspicuous space.

Make icing by adding extract to powdered sugar. Add buttermilk, a little at the time, until the icing is thick but pourable.

Divide among 3 small bowls. Color 1 bowl purple, 1 green, and 1 gold.

Drizzle over cake. Add sprinkles.

Icing:

2 cups powdered sugar
4–5 tablespoons buttermilk
½ teaspoon almond or orange extract

Gel coloring and sprinkles
Small plastic baby

Chocolate-Covered Cream-Filled Whole Wheat Biscuits

Yield: 12

Preheat oven to 450°

When I tasted the first batch of Honey Whole Wheat biscuits (see page 39), I was surprised by how closely the taste resembled graham crackers. I had never given much thought to the ingredients in graham crackers but, when I researched it, I discovered that the honey whole wheat biscuits I just made were essentially fluffy graham crackers. Composing a cream-filled sandwich with the graham cracker–like biscuits seemed the perfect course to take. Something reminiscent of MoonPies would be delightful and give me an opportunity to pay homage to a wonderful Southern company, Chattanooga Bakery, and their product, MoonPie, that has been a part of our culture for generations. My earliest memory of MoonPie, was its daily inclusion in my granddaddy's sack lunch that he carried to work at the cotton mill in Geneva, Alabama. Fast forward to the early 1960s when my family moved to Mobile, Alabama, the original Mardi Gras city in the United States. Then, as it still is today, MoonPie is a favorite Mardi Gras throw. Paradegoers of all ages yell to the revelers, "Hey Mister, throw me a MoonPie!"

I experimented with different recipes for cream filling before settling on the plain store-bought version. My marshmallow recipe, which I use each year at Christmas, makes beautiful marshmallows that everyone enjoys, but the texture is a little too firm for a cream filling. The next try was using store-bought marshmallow cream and embellishing it with powdered sugar, butter, and vanilla extract. The flavor was good and the texture creamy, but it didn't hold up at room temperature. So, the best version is the marshmallow cream straight from the jar.

Biscuit:

12 Honey Whole Wheat biscuits no larger than 2 inches across. (See recipe page 39)

Filling:

7 ounces jar marshmallow crème

Chocolate coating:

16 ounces milk chocolate
½ bar paraffin wax
1 tablespoon heavy cream

Split biscuits in half. Spread a teaspoon of filling on the inside half of the biscuit and top with the other half. Secure with a toothpick. Repeat until all biscuits are filled. You may have more filling than you need. Place filled biscuits on a baking sheet and freeze for 1 hour. Do not remove toothpick yet.

For chocolate coating, melt all ingredients over a double boiler.

To assemble:

Remove 2 or 3 biscuits at the time from the freezer. Working quickly, dip biscuit in chocolate and coat well. If your pot is shallow, hold the biscuit over the pot of melted chocolate and spoon chocolate over it. Place chocolate-covered biscuit on waxed paper. Repeat until all are covered.

Let dry.

My grandmother would consider tassies a waste of time. She would have made a pecan pie and be done with it.

Tassies and Pecan Pies

The first I heard of Tassies was in Nathalie Dupree's cookbook, *Southern Memories*. She recounts a luncheon she prepared for the mother of the gentleman she was seeing. She used her good linen, china, and flower vases to ensure beauty and charm throughout the meal. The woman was delighted by the Pecan Tassies (miniature pecan pies) Nathalie had chosen for dessert. Nathalie's description of the setting was dreamy and sophisticated. I had no doubt her social circles were very different from those of my family. My mother lacked confidence in her ability to entertain gracefully. In reality, she possessed a great deal of charm and social graces. My grandmother was much too practical to entertain in a way she described as "putting on the dog." She was never fortunate enough to own fine china and linens. Besides, all the work that went into Pecan Tassies would be deemed unnecessary in her eyes. She would make a whole Pecan Pie and be done with it. Two different worlds entirely, and I'm fortunate to have lived in both.

Buttermilk Blueberry Tassies

Yield: 24

Preheat oven to 350°

The crust for Tassies had the necessary ingredients for biscuits: flour, fat, and dairy. The dairy is in the form of cream cheese. The inspiration for the filling came from an article my daughter sent me highlighting a recipe for Buttermilk Blueberry Pie. Our blueberry bushes were producing a bumper crop, and Buttermilk Pie is something I make frequently. I think that was her way of telling me she'd like me to make her a Buttermilk Pie and throw in some of our freshly picked blueberries. So, I whittled down my buttermilk pie recipe to the amount of filling I thought I needed for the 24 Tassies and used some of our freshly picked blueberries.

Crust:

½ cup unsalted butter, room temperature
4 ounces cream cheese, room temperature

1 cup all-purpose flour

Filling

2 eggs, separated
½ cup sugar
1½ tablespoons self-rising flour

2 tablespoons unsalted butter, melted
1 cup buttermilk
72 uncooked blueberries

For crust:

Spray a 24-cup mini muffin pan with nonstick spray.

Using an electric mixer, cream butter and cream cheese until smooth. Add in flour and beat until combined.

Turn out the dough onto a lightly floured surface. Shape into a ball. Sprinkle with a little flour if the dough is sticky. Divide the dough in half. Roll each half into a 6-inch log. Divide each log into 12 pieces and shape each piece into a small ball. Place one ball in each cup of the muffin tin. Press the dough evenly on the bottom and sides of each cup.

Repeat process with the remaining dough.

Chill the dough in the muffin cup for at least 1 hour.

For filling:

Add egg yolks to a large mixer bowl and beat until fluffy.

Mix together flour and sugar.

Add flour mixture to egg yolks and beat with electric mixer until mixed well.

Add buttermilk and melted butter to egg mixture and beat until mixed well.

Beat egg whites until fluffy and fold into filling.

To assemble:

Place two blueberries into each muffin cup.

Fill muffin cups with custard filling, approximately 1 tablespoon per cup.

Top the filling in each cup with the remaining blueberries.

Bake at 350° for 40 minutes or until the tops are browned and the filling is set.

Remove from oven. Let cool 10 minutes.

The tassies need some gentle coaxing to come out of the tins. Gently run a knife along the edge of each cup and then carefully remove each tassie. They are dainty little things and must be handled as such.

Resurrection Biscuits

Yield: 8

Preheat oven to 400°

Make a dessert with your kids and teach them the Resurrection story at the same time. Using canned biscuits and large marshmallows, this is a cooking project that will remind you of Vacation Bible School. I still remember some of the fun crafts I made as a child in VBS. Plan this activity for Easter and let the Resurrection story come alive for your child. This activity explains the miracle of the resurrection as well as a sermon. I first became aware of this recipe when a typewritten copy was mistakenly mixed in with some of my work papers. I had forgotten about it until my friend, Dawn, asked me if I had ever heard of it. I researched online and found the recipe all over creation with no attribution to the original source. The copy I received used canned crescent rolls, as do most of the recipes online. Canned biscuits work just as well. Brushing the tops of the biscuits with melted butter and sprinkling with cinnamon sugar is my addition and isn't symbolic of the story. It simply makes the biscuits taste better.

1 tablespoon granulated sugar
2 teaspoons ground cinnamon
8 large canned biscuits
8 large marshmallows
2 tablespoons melted butter, cooled

Mix sugar and cinnamon in a small bowl.

Make 1 biscuit at the time. Press a biscuit as flat as you can get it with the back of your hand.

Dip 1 marshmallow in melted butter and coat well. Then, roll the marshmallow in the cinnamon sugar mixture until well coated.

Place the coated marshmallow on the inside of the biscuit near the edge. Roll the biscuit up and around the marshmallow 1 half turn. Fold in the edges of the biscuit. Finish rolling. Pinch seams and place seam-side down on a baking sheet that has been greased or covered in a baking mat. Make sure seams are pinched together well or the marshmallow will leak out.

Repeat the process with the other 7 biscuits.

Brush tops of the biscuits with the remaining butter and sprinkle with cinnamon sugar.

Bake in a 400° preheat oven for 12 minutes or until the biscuit is golden brown.

Remove from the oven and let cool about 5 minutes.

Cut into the biscuit and you'll find the marshmallow has disappeared!

Here's the symbolism:
Biscuit – the cloth they wrapped Jesus in when they buried him
Marshmallow – Jesus's body
Butter – embalming oils
Cinnamon sugar – spices used to prepare Jesus's body for burial
Baked biscuit – empty tomb
For scripture reference, read John 20:1-8 while the biscuits are baking.

Biscuits in a Biscuit Shop

The popularity of biscuits has created entrepreneurial opportunities. Biscuits shops are springing up all over, particularly in the Northeast. It seems folks are finally catching on to what Southerners have known all along: biscuits are practical, biscuits are good eating, and biscuits are light and flaky yet sturdy. Biscuits are perfect! The menus in biscuit shops vary from traditional biscuit offerings to modern-day creations using trendy ingredients.

The Andy Griffith Show tin is one of my favorites in my tin collection.

Lunch in the Drugstore

In addition to dispensing medication prescriptions, mega retail chain pharmacies today are mini-markets where you can buy everything from school supplies to dishwashing detergent. There was a time in small-town America when pharmacists not only dispensed the medication, but they also owned the drugstore. And typical of so many small business owners, they knew their customers. A visit to the drugstore was a social event. The pharmacist would ask about your family, and you would want to know about his. The best feature of the drugstore was the soda fountain where you could get ice cream cones, milkshakes, pie, sandwiches, and fountain cokes. To a Southerner, the term *coke* was generic for soft drinks. If you ordered a coke, more than likely, you'd be asked, "What kind?" And that didn't mean diet or regular. It meant Coca-Cola, Dr. Pepper, 7-up, orange, grape, Pepsi, or Cherry Coca-Cola.

My favorite lunch counter meal was a chicken salad sandwich and Coca-Cola. The sandwich was filled with chicken salad made the old-fashioned way: cooked chicken, mayonnaise, celery, boiled eggs, and pickle relish served wrapped in wax paper. You may have been served a pickle spear or some chips alongside, but usually it was just the sandwich. While I enjoy fancy chicken salad made with nuts and fruits, I still prefer the old-fashioned kind. This is the way my mother and grandmother made chicken salad. The only way I deviate from their method is by roasting the chicken instead of boiling it, which results in more flavorful chicken. Chicken salad is a part of Southern culture. I'm fairly certain it's against the law to host a bridal shower or ladies luncheon and not serve it.

Drugstore lunch counters are slowly disappearing. Independently owned drugstores are finding it hard to compete with retail pharmacy chains. Along with the loss of drugstore lunch counters is the loss of a way of life that was slower, simpler, and kinder. I long for the day that I can locate a town like Mayberry in *The Andy Griffith Show*. We've seen every episode of the show's eight seasons and we continue to watch them. I guess you might say we're groupies. We're drawn to that era and that way of life. Somewhere out there is a town similar to Mayberry. If it's meant to be, we'll find it. And, when we do, I'm ordering a chicken salad sandwich and a coke in the drugstore.

Old-Fashioned Chicken Salad on Yogurt Biscuit Bread

Yield: four sandwiches

I put chicken salad in two categories: fancy and old-fashioned. Fancy may have fresh herbs, grapes, apples, pecans, or almonds. While I enjoy most any combination for chicken salad, my favorite is old-fashioned made the simple way my mother and grandmother made it.

4 cups cooked chicken, cut in ½-inch cubes
½–¾ cup good quality mayonnaise
2 boiled eggs, peeled and diced
2 tablespoons finely minced celery
¼ cup sweet pickle relish
Salt and ground black pepper to taste
1 batch Yogurt Biscuit Bread, cut in 4-inch squares (see recipe page 62)
Lettuce greens

Mix all ingredients. Taste for seasoning and adjust. Chill.

To assemble:

Split Yogurt Biscuits Bread Squares (see recipe page 62). Fill with chicken salad. Place greens on top of salad.

Ham Biscuits

with Honey Mustard Butter

Yield: Approximately 12 (2½-inch) biscuits or approximately 20 (1¾-inch) biscuits

Southern hams are cured by sugar or salt. Most commercially cured hams use a sugar cure method and are sometimes called city hams in contrast with country hams, which are salt-cured. Of course, sugar-cured hams are sweeter, but the flavor is milder. You can stack as much sugar-cured ham in a biscuit as you'd like. Care must be taken with country ham and only small portions should be used. These biscuits are filled with sugar-cured ham topped with honey mustard butter. For breakfast biscuits, cut biscuits with a 2½-inch biscuit cutter. For appetizers, use a 1¾-inch biscuit cutter. Ham biscuits are a popular appetizer and will be one of the first to go. They may be served warm or room temperature. Folks like them either way.

½ cup unsalted butter, softened
1 tablespoon honey Dijon mustard
Buttermilk biscuits (see recipe page 29)
½–¾ pound sugar-cured ham

Mix butter, mustard, and honey until smooth.

Cut ham to the appropriate size to fit the biscuits. Split the biscuits and divide ham evenly among the number of biscuits you want to make. Spread butter on the underside of the biscuit top.

Turkey on Sour Cream and Chive Biscuits

Yield: approximately 12 (2-½ inch) biscuits

Leftover cold turkey comes alive when put into a sandwich with flavorful sour cream and chive biscuits. This would be a welcomed change of pace after Thanksgiving, when you feel like you can't bear to eat one more turkey sandwich. A good deli turkey can be used, also.

½ cup mayonnaise
1 teaspoon Dijon type mustard
½ teaspoon seasoned salt
¼ cup finely chopped flat leaf parsley
Sour Cream and Chive Drop Biscuits, split (see recipe on page 57)
Sliced turkey
Mixed greens

Mix together first 4 ingredients and set aside. Assemble sandwiches by spreading a thin layer of mayonnaise on the inside of both biscuit pieces. Fill with turkey and top with mixed greens.

Ham, Egg, and Cheddar Cheese Biscuit Cupcakes

Yield: 6

Preheat oven to 350°

This recipe calls for sugar-cured ham, not its salty cousin, country ham. Brown the ham to bring out maximum flavor before adding eggs. The addition of buttermilk to the eggs adds flavor to them and keeps them moist. I whipped up this on a whim on a Monday morning. Sometimes, my whims work out, sometimes they don't. This one is a winner and would make a fine breakfast any day of the week. For busy weekday mornings, they can be baked ahead of time, stored in the refrigerator, and reheated. I recommend wrapping them securely in aluminum foil and reheating on 350° for 10 minutes or until heated through. For especially busy mornings, they are an excellent grab-n-go breakfast.

Biscuit cups:

1 cup self-rising flour
¼ cup butter, cubed and chilled
½ cup buttermilk

Filling:

½ cup sugar-cured ham, ¼-inch dice
6 eggs
1 tablespoon buttermilk

¼ teaspoon salt
$1/8$ teaspoon ground pepper
1½ cups grated sharp cheddar cheese, divided

For biscuit cups:

Add flour to bowl. Cut or rub in butter until flour resembles coarse meal. Pour in buttermilk and stir until dough is wet.

Turn out onto a floured surface. Sprinkle flour on dough. Knead gently and add flour, as needed, until dough is no longer sticky.

Roll out into a rectangle ½ inch thick. Cut with a 2½-inch biscuit cutter dipped in flour.

Place biscuits in a standard-sized cupcake pan that brushed with cooking oil. Press dough up sides of each cup until the cup is entirely covered with biscuit dough. Prick bottom of each biscuit a few times with a fork. Set aside.

For filling:

Brown ham in a skillet coated with cooking oil.

Whisk together eggs, buttermilk, salt, and pepper until the eggs are light.

Add egg mixture to ham. Cook eggs until soft scrambled.

Remove from heat. Stir in 1 cup cheese.

Divide egg mixture among the biscuit cups.

Top with remaining cheddar cheese.

Bake in a 350° oven for 25 minutes or until cheese melts and eggs are firmly set.

Roast Beef Sandwich
with Mustard Sauce on Yogurt Biscuit Bread

Yield: 4 sandwiches

Thinly sliced roast beef, arugula, mustard sauce, and yogurt biscuit bread make an outstanding sandwich.

2 tablespoons good quality mayonnaise
1 teaspoon sour cream
1 tablespoon mustard, choose your favorite
1 teaspoon honey
1 batch Yogurt Biscuit Bread (see recipe page 62)
12 ounces thinly sliced deli roast beef
Baby arugula
½ sweet onion, sliced

Mustard sauce:

Mix first four ingredients. Set aside.

To assemble:

Slice biscuit bread in half. Spread mustard sauce on inside of top and bottom. Divide roast beef among the sandwiches. Top with arugula and sliced onions. Replace bread top on sandwich.

Grilled Peach Salad
with Rosemary Focaccia Biscuit Bread

Yield: 4 servings

Peaches and rosemary make a surprisingly beautiful couple. They were made for each other. If the combination is an acquired taste, then I've bought it lock, stock, and barrel. Rosemary focaccia bread and grilled peach salad is a lunch I could eat every day. Peaches have two classifications: clingstone and freestone. Freestone peaches are easier to cut in half because the flesh easily separates from the stone.

Grilled peaches:

Peel 2 peaches and slice in half. Place them cut-side down on a hot grill. Cook until grill marks show, about 1 to 2 minutes per side.

Remove from grill and slice.

To assemble salad:

8 cups arugula greens
Olive oil
Kosher salt
Grilled peaches
Blue cheese sprinkles

Lightly dress arugula leaves with olive oil and salt. Toss. Divide among 4 plates.

Place ½ grilled peach, sliced, in the center of dressed greens. Add a few blue cheese sprinkles to salad. Drizzle honey over peaches.

Serve with Rosemary Focaccia Biscuit Bread (see recipe page 65).

My collection of vintage spools and bobbins used in textile mills.

A Cotton Mill Worker's Lunch

After my grandparents almost starved to death trying to make a living farming, they decided Granddaddy should try to "get on" at the newly built cotton mill. After he was hired, they moved from the tenant's house provided by the landowner for whom they sharecropped and moved to the cotton mill village where they provided housing for the workers. Houses in the mill village were small and would be considered substandard today. They were sturdily built and provided running water and shelter from the elements. Eventually, they got electricity. At first, the only heat was a small coal stove, which was upgraded to a kerosene furnace. It was the place my grandparents lived for the twenty-five-plus years Granddaddy worked at the mill.

The mill whistle signaled six alarms each day. *Blasted* is a more appropriate word. The village and the entire town heard the whistles. The first whistle would blow at ten minutes before the shift. The next whistle blew at shift time: 6:00 a.m., 2:00 p.m., and 10:00 p.m. There was no excuse for anyone sleeping through the whistle unless they were stone cold deaf or dead.

Granddaddy worked the 6:00 a.m. shift, which meant the day started early at their house. Granny would start rattling pots and pans as Granddaddy put on his overalls. Biscuits were made every morning so Granddaddy could eat his traditional breakfast of cane syrup–sopped biscuits. For lunch, Granny cooked two eggs hard and made two biscuit sandwiches, which she wrapped in waxed paper and placed in a brown paper sack. On top of the biscuit sandwiches, she would slide in a MoonPie or occasionally a Little Debbie cake. This seemingly light lunch fueled my Granddaddy as he worked a job that required hard labor. The job was hard, but it paid him a regular wage that wasn't affected by weather, pests, floods, or droughts. He was mighty proud to have it.

Bacon Cathead Biscuit

with Fried Egg and American Cheese

Yield: 4 biscuits

For breakfast or lunch, this biscuit sandwich is comforting and spirit lifting. The flavors are familiar and simple. This isn't the kind of sandwich you bite into and have to take several more bites before you can decide if you like it. Chances are, you like it at first sight. The first bite will seal the deal.

4 Bacon Cathead Biscuits (see recipe page 61)
2 tablespoons bacon drippings
4 eggs
4 slices American cheese

Place bacon drippings in a large skillet and heat to medium. Add eggs and fry until yolks are to your desired degree of doneness.

Split biscuits in half. Place an egg and slice of cheese on 1 half of the biscuit and top with the other half.

Loaded Baked Potato Biscuit

Yield: 4

Preheat oven to 450°

Our society is crazy for the flavor of loaded baked potato. In addition to an actual baked potato loaded with butter, sour cream, chives, bacon, and cheddar cheese, we carry the theme over to potato skins, potato chips, casseroles, and soups. So, why not a biscuit? I couldn't think of a reason to not do it, either. I used a Yukon gold potato because I wanted a smooth texture with less starch. Instead of mashing the potato, I cut it into small diced pieces that can be seen in the biscuit.

2 cups self-rising winter wheat flour

½ cup butter, unsalted, cubed and chilled

3 tablespoons fresh chives, finely chopped

8 ounces sour cream

1 medium potato, baked, cooled and peeled (approximately 4–6 ounces)

1–2 tablespoons buttermilk, if needed

4–6 ounces sharp cheddar cheese, grated

4 slices bacon, cooked until crispy. Reserve bacon drippings

Place flour in a large bowl. Rub or cut in butter until the flour resembles coarse meal. Stir in chives and sour cream.

Cut the peeled, cooled potato into small diced pieces. Stir into dough. Add buttermilk, if needed, until the dough is wet.

Turn out onto a floured surface and shape into a 1-inch thick rectangle. If dough is too sticky to handle, sprinkle with flour.

Cut biscuits with a 2½-inch cutter dipped in flour. Place 1 inch apart on a baking sheet sprayed with a nonstick spray or covered with a baking mat.

Brush tops with bacon drippings.

Bake in a preheated 450° oven for 15 to 18 minutes or until the tops are golden brown.

Let cool 5 minutes. Split in half and place on a baking sheet. Divide the cheese among the 8 biscuits halves. Place a piece of bacon on top of the cheese that's on the bottom half of each biscuit. Broil until cheese melts. Cover the bottom half of the biscuit with the top half.

Serve immediately.

Loaded Baked Potato Biscuit

Biscuits in a Butler's Pantry

A trend in new home building today is the return of a butler's pantry with the intended purpose of a food staging area. I've never lived in a house with a butler's pantry. For those who have one, I wonder how many times it's used for the intended purpose versus a catch-all storage room. Regardless, I love the nostalgia.

Entertaining is as common in our Southern culture as grits. We love to feed people at any time of the day or night. Whether it's a party, an informal gathering of friends and family, or a visit from a neighbor, we will bang some pots and pans and fix something to eat. The offerings in this chapter can be used for an appetizer, first course, or light meal.

Pigs in a Biscuit Blanket 126

Supreme Pizza Pull-Apart Bread 129

Barbequed Country-style Rib Fried Hand Pie 130

Salmon Chive Patties on Dill Biscuits 134

Brandied Apricot Jam and Goat Cheese with Tavern Biscuits 137

Spicy Pimento Cheese Bites 138

Skillet Toasted Biscuits with Herb Cream Cheese and Country Tomato Relish 140

Pigs in a Biscuit Blanket

Yield: 75 to 80 pieces

Wrap little beef or pork smoked cocktail sausages in a garlic cheese biscuit blanket and serve it with Jezebel Sauce, a traditional sweet Southern cocktail sauce that gets a kick from horseradish. These pick-ups, traditionally made with crescent rolls dough, are always some of the first to go at party. Impress your guests by dressing them up and adding a new twist.

Making fresh biscuit dough, rolling it out, and cutting strips requires a little more effort than using canned crescent roll dough, but it pays off in spades. Don't stress over-calculating the dimensions of the dough to get the right amount of strips. The dough is rather forgiving and each strip can be manipulated to result in the size needed to wrap the sausage. Unless you are precise and measure each strip, there will be a little variation in size. I think that is perfectly lovely and has the look of something made by hand. When it comes time to wrap the sausages in dough, recruit anyone you can get your hands on to help wrap all the piggies in their biscuit blankets.

One batch Garlic Cheese Biscuits (see recipe page 45)
2 (13- or 14-ounce) packages fully cooked smoked cocktail sausages
Sesame seeds

Prepare biscuit dough and roll to ¼-inch thick in a rectangle approximately 10 inches by 22 inches. Cut out enough strips, about 1 inch by 2 inches, to wrap each sausage.

Make certain sausages are well drained and dry before wrapping.

Take 1 strip, dip in flour if sticky, and fold in half lengthwise. Then, press the dough, strip out, to 3 inches in length. I used my index finger as a guide. Wrap the sausage with the dough strip, making sure to overlap the dough. Place seam-side down on a baking sheet sprayed with a nonstick spray or covered with a baking mat.

Repeat with remaining dough and sausages until all are wrapped, placing them 1 inch apart on the baking sheet.

Brush tops with oil or spray with nonstick spray and sprinkle with sesame seeds.

Bake in a preheated 400° oven for 20 minutes or until tops are lightly browned.

Serve with Jezebel Sauce.

Jezebel Sauce

This sauce makes a wonderful ham glaze, too.

1 (18-ounce) jar pineapple preserves
1 (18-ounce) jar apple jelly
1 (5.25-ounce) jar prepared horseradish

3 tablespoons dry mustard
1–2 teaspoons coarsely ground black pepper
1 tablespoon honey

Mix with an electric mixer. Refrigerate leftovers.

Pigs in a Biscuit Blanket

Supreme Pizza Pull-Apart Bread

Yield: One loaf

All the flavors of a supreme pizza are captured and put together with pull-apart bread made easy by using canned biscuits. This bread makes entertaining fun and is a welcome change from carry-out pizza.

2 tablespoons cooking oil
½ cup diced sweet onion
½ cup diced sweet pepper
½ cup diced fresh mushrooms
½ pound sweet Italian sausage

4 (7.5-ounce) cans buttermilk biscuits
4 ounces pepperoni, roughly chopped
3 ounces Canadian bacon, diced
2 cups shredded mozzarella cheese
1 cup grated Parmesan cheese

Heat a large skillet to medium high and add oil. Sauté onions, peppers, and mushrooms until soft.

Add Italian sausage to skillet. Crumble and brown until pink is gone. Drain if needed. Set aside to cool while you prepare the biscuits.

Cut biscuits in half and add to a super-sized bowl. Add remaining ingredients and stir or mix well with your hands.

Pour mixture into a tube pan sprayed with nonstick spray.

Cover a sheet pan with aluminum foil. Place tube pan on sheet pan. Some of the grease may leak through the pan and the covered sheet pan will catch it.

Bake in a 350° preheated oven for 50 to 60 minutes or until center is done. Let cool for 10 minutes before removing from pan. Serve with marinara sauce for dipping.

Barbequed Country-style Rib Fried Hand Pie

Yield: 20 (3½-inch) oblong fried pies

*Natchitoches (pronounced nak-uh-dush) Meat Pies were made famous by the movie **Steel Magnolia.** They are handheld fried pies filled with seasoned ground beef and pork. Fried pies, or hand pies, are nothing new. Southerners have been making sweet, fruit-filled fried pies for generations. Savory fried pies aren't quite as common. Taking inspiration from the Natchitoches pies, I used leftover barbequed Southern-style rib meat to create a handpie that will serve as party appetizer or first course. Surprisingly, the pies have a better taste at room temperature than hot from the fry pan. This makes them an even better choice as a party appetizer. Don't drizzle on barbecue sauce until right before eating.*

2 cups cooked barbequed country-style rib meat, finely chopped
1 batch Buttermilk Biscuits★
Cooking oil, enough for 1-inch deep in cooking vessel
Barbecue sauce for garnish

★For buttermilk biscuits, see page 29. Follow recipe down to folding technique. After the dough is folded, roll out to ½ inch thick.

With buttermilk biscuit dough rolled to ½ inch thick, cut out 20 biscuits with a 3-inch biscuit cutter. Pat out each biscuit with your hand until slightly flat.

Divide the chopped rib meat among the biscuit, placing it in the center of each. I put roughly a scant kitchen teaspoonful on each biscuit.

Dip your finger and water and moisten the outside edge. This helps the biscuit stay folded after crimping.

Fold each biscuit in half. Be sure to tuck the meat inside as you fold.

Crimp the folded edge.

In a cooking vessel with high sides, heat 1 inch of cooking oil to 350°.

Drop in the biscuits in batches, being careful not to overcrowd. Fry on one side, about 3 minutes, until golden brown. Flip and fry about 3 minutes on the other side.

Remove to a draining rack. Repeat with remainder of the biscuits.

Drizzle with barbecue sauce before eating.

Barbequed Country-style Rib Fried Hand Pie

I hope my grandchildren have fond food memories that involve me.

Sal-mon Patties

grew up hearing the "L" pronounced in salmon. That remains a common pronunciation in rural parts of the Deep South where some folks are adamant that it's the correct and only way to pronounce it. Besides, whoever took the "L" away made one more word that school children can't spell phonetically.

Salmon patties were a staple in my grandmother and mother's kitchens. Canned salmon was accessible and inexpensive. Throwing together salmon patties made quick work of getting dinner on the table. We would eat the patty with ketchup along with a couple of side dishes, or make a sandwich with mayonnaise and ketchup on white bread. I've heard salmon patties referred to as Poor Man's Crab Cakes. My family didn't consider them a substitute for crab cakes because they didn't feel the need to have anything as elaborate as crab cakes as part of our routine meals. Before fresh fish or a variety of quality frozen fish was available in Southern groceries, sitting down to a fish meal meant you or someone you know had been fishing. Canned salmon was relied upon as a way to bring fish to the table when the fishermen were down on their luck.

One of my fondest food memories involves my grandmother and salmon patties. We finished hanging out the clothes on the clothesline and went into the kitchen to make lunch, which she called dinner. She started cooking salmon patties and pulled out a recipe she had just received for an egg custard pie that she called a magic pie because it made its own crust. I was old enough, she thought, to learn how to make this pie. As she cooked the salmon patties, she coaxed me through the pie-making process. She thought the combination of salmon patties and egg custard pie made for an extraordinarily special lunch. It made an extraordinarily lunch, alright, but in a different way than she imagined.

Salmon Chive Patties on Dill Biscuits

Yield: 8 appetizers or first course servings

This is an updated version of my grandmother's salmon patty recipe, which I turned into an appetizer or first course and serve with dill biscuits. Instead of finely chopped onion, I substituted fresh chives. She ordinarily added flour as a binder, although, I have seen her crush up a sleeve of saltine crackers to use instead of flour. I used bread crumbs instead. Leftover biscuits pulsed in the food processor until they are crumbs could be used. Thinly sliced radishes are optional, but they do add a nice crunchy texture to the dish.

For Dill Biscuits, see recipe page49

Salmon patties:

1 (7½-ounce) can wild Alaskan pink salmon, drained

1 egg, slightly beaten

3 tablespoons finely chopped fresh chives

3 tablespoons plain breadcrumbs

1 teaspoon seasoned salt

Cooking oil for frying

Sauce:

1 tablespoon apple cider vinegar

2 tablespoon mayonnaise★

1 teaspoon granulated sugar

¼ teaspoon ground black pepper

★I use Duke's mayonnaise, which contains no sugar. If using a different brand, the amount of sugar might need adjusting.

For salmon patties:

Add salmon, egg, and chives to a mixing bowl. Stir together.

In a small bowl, stir breadcrumbs and seasoned salt. Add to salmon mixture and stir.

Divide into 8 portions and form patties about 2 inches wide and ¼ inches thick.

Over medium-high heat, fry patties three to four minutes or until golden brown. Flip over and repeat on other side.

Remove from skillet and drain on paper towel.

For Sauce:

Whisk together.

To assemble:

Split open biscuits. Spread sauce on both sides. Add salmon patty one side and top with a thinly sliced radish. Top with other half of biscuit.

Salmon Chive Patties on Dill Biscuits

Brandied Apricot Jam and Goat Cheese
with Tavern Biscuits

Yield: 6 to 8 appetizer servings

I found Mrs. Dull's Tavern Biscuits so interesting, I wanted to come up with a way to use them on a cheese board in the same manner as crackers. While they're slightly sweet, the flat appearance and tiny holes make them favor crackers more than modern biscuits. A tangy cheese, such as goat cheese, would offset the sweetness of the biscuit. Brandied apricot jam would complement the brandy in the biscuits. Since apricots were out of season, I experimented with dried apricots to make the jam, but I could never get it just right. Adding brandy to a good-quality commercially prepared apricot jam and heating produced the desired results.

½ cup quality apricot jam
1 tablespoon brandy
4 ounces goat cheese
Tavern biscuits (see page 47)

Add apricot jam and brandy to a small sauce pan. Heat until the jam melts, stirring occasionally. Remove from heat and chill before using.

To serve, top the cheese with a small amount of jam and spread on tavern biscuits.

Spicy Pimento Cheese Bites

Yield: about 15

Preheat oven to 450°

I felt compelled to have a pimento cheese (we say pimmenocheese) recipe lest I forsake my Southern heritage. Kids in the South are raised on pimento cheese sandwiches. The Master's, a prestigious PGA major golf tournament held at the famous Augusta National Golf Club, has a long-standing pimento cheese sandwich tradition. A favorite childhood lunch for me was pimmenocheese on toasted white bread with pink lemonade. For some reason, I preferred pink lemonade over regular even though there's no difference in the taste, only color. From kitchen sandwiches to major golf tournaments and everything in between, we are pimento cheese people. For this recipe, use your favorite homemade pimento cheese or purchase a quality store-bought variety.

Placing the jalapeño slice on top of the pimento cheese instead of under it gives the pepper slice a little time to roast, which adds flavor and brings out a little sweetness.

¾ cup soft winter wheat all-purpose flour
1¼ teaspoons baking powder
¼ teaspoon kosher salt
¼ cup plain cornmeal

¼ cup unsalted butter, cubed and chilled
½ cup buttermilk
½–¾ cups pimento cheese
15 pickled jalapeño pepper slices

Place flour, baking powder, kosher salt, and cornmeal in a bowl and stir lightly. Rub or cut in butter until flour resembles coarse meal.

Pour in buttermilk and stir until dough is wet and sticky. Turn out onto a well-floured surface. Sprinkle flour on top. Gently work in the flour, adding more as needed, until the dough is no longer sticky and holds its shape.

Roll out to ½ inch thick. Cut with a 2-inch biscuit cutter dipped in flour.

With the back of your hand, flatten out the cut-out biscuit as much as possible.

Spray a mini-muffin pan with nonstick spray.

Place about a teaspoon of pimento cheese in the center of the biscuit cut out. Press the edges of the cut out toward the center to form a flower shape. Place the biscuit in a mini-muffin cup and top with a pickled jalapeño slice.

Repeat with each biscuit cut out.

Place in a 450° oven for 12 minutes or until the cheese is melted and slightly brown and the biscuit is done.

Remove from oven and transfer each biscuit to a cooling rack for 5 minutes. Best served warm.

Spicy Pimento Cheese Bites

Skillet Toasted Biscuits

with Herb Cream Cheese and Country Tomato Relish

Yield: 16 biscuit halves

As much as we love our biscuits and eat them regularly, there's bound to be some left over. You can always throw them in a freezer bag and keep adding until you have enough to make a pan of dressing to accompany a roasted chicken or the Thanksgiving turkey. Skillet toasting is another way to make use of a biscuit after it's lost its freshness. Use any savory biscuit that you have on hand. Herb cream cheese topped with a country tomato relish adds wonderful texture and flavor to the biscuit toasted crispy in bacon drippings.

Country tomato relish:

2 tablespoon bacon drippings
1 medium sweet onion, finely chopped
1 (14.5-ounce) can diced tomatoes
2 tablespoons fresh basil, roughly chopped

1 tablespoon honey
2 tablespoons pickled jalapeño slices, finely
 chopped
Salt and pepper to taste

Skillet toasted biscuits:

6 slices uncooked bacon

8 leftover biscuits, split open

Cream cheese spread:

8 ounces cream cheese, softened
2 heaping tablespoons mayonnaise

1 tablespoon fresh dill, finely chopped
1 tablespoon fresh chives, finely chopped

For country tomato relish:

Add bacon drippings to a medium-sized cast-iron skillet over medium heat. Add onion and cook until tender and translucent, about 15 minutes.

Add tomatoes and their juice. Continue over medium heat until most of the liquid has evaporated.

Stir in basil, honey, and jalapeño peppers. Cook until basil has wilted.

Taste for seasonings and adjust.

Set aside.

For skillet toasted biscuits:

Cook bacon in large cast-iron skillet over medium heat. Remove when crispy and drain on paper towels.

While the skillet is still hot, put in the biscuits cut-side down. When toasted brown, flip over and repeat on the other side. You may need to cook in batches.

Set biscuits aside.

To assemble:

Spread cut side of biscuits with cream cheese spread. Top with a dollop of tomato relish. Crumble bacon over biscuits.

Biscuits in Everyday Home Meals

It's easy to imagine biscuits as part of a meal. They're most often thought of as bread that's eaten alongside the meal. Biscuits are capable of playing various roles at the family dinner table. They can be croutons for soup, dressing for poultry, crusts for pies and pizza, or toppings for meat casseroles. The ease and quickness of preparation encourages their use for all meals, even quick weeknight meals to accommodate busy schedules.

Homemade Tomato Soup with Cheddar Cheese Thyme Biscuit Croutons 145

Cornish Game Hens with Cornbread Biscuit and Giblet Dressing 147

Breakfast Pizza with Biscuit Crust 150

Hamburger Pot Pie with Herb Biscuit Topper 152

Pepperoni Pizza with Biscuit Crust 154

Summer Vegetable Pie with Cheese Garlic Biscuit Crust 157

Barbecue Pork on Mashed Potato Biscuit with Cajun Crispy Fried Onions 159

Grilled Salad with Biscuit Croutons 163

Chicken and Dumplings 168

Homemade Tomato Soup

with Cheddar Cheese Thyme Biscuit Croutons

Yield: 4 to 6 servings

I ate plenty of tomato soup as a kid. It was a staple at our house. The kind that I ate was opened with a can opener and had cute little kids on the label. Homemade tomato soup entered my life later. It's so much a favorite now that I keep quality canned diced tomatoes and tomato sauce on hand in my pantry just to have tomato soup when the craving hits. The sodium content in this recipe is sufficient for our taste and, therefore, I didn't use additional salt.

When adding fresh thyme to soups or stews, I don't bother to strip off those tiny leaves. Tie several sprigs with kitchen twine and remove them before serving. The leaves will fall off naturally while cooking.

2 tablespoons cooking oil
2 sweet onions, diced
2 medium carrots, peeled and diced
2 cloves garlic minced
2 (14.5-ounce) cans diced tomatoes
1 (15-ounce) can tomato sauce

1 quart chicken stock
Few sprigs fresh thyme
1 tablespoon honey
½ teaspoon fresh ground black pepper
2 tablespoons half-and-half

Heat a large pot to medium high. Add cooking oil and onions and carrots. Cook until soft, about 10 to 15 minutes. Add garlic and cook an additional 2 minutes.

Pour in tomatoes, tomato sauce, chicken stock, sprigs of thyme, honey, and black pepper.

Cover, cook over medium heat for 30 minutes.

Remove thyme sprigs. Purée using an immersion blender. Stir in half-and-half.

Garnish with Cheddar Cheese Thyme Biscuits Croutons. Recipe found on following page.

Cheddar Cheese Thyme Biscuits Croutons

Bake croutons until they are crispier and browner than you would biscuits. They can be made earlier in the day and left out to harden a tad, which will keep them from getting soggy too quickly in the soup. The amount of grated cheese will make the dough somewhat lumpy and bumpy. You'll have a hearty cheese flavored crouton that will complement the soup nicely. Ordinarily, I brush the tops of biscuits with oil after they're cut and on the baking sheet. For little croutons, I find it easier to brush the dough after it's rolled out. Be sure to brush the wheel of the pizza cutter, too.

1 cup soft winter wheat self-rising flour
¼ cup unsalted butter, cubed and chilled
1½ cups sharp cheddar cheese, grated
2 teaspoons fresh thyme leaves
½ cup buttermilk

Put flour in bowl and cut or rub in butter until flour resembles coarse dough. Stir in cheese and thyme. Add buttermilk and stir until dough is wet.

Turn dough out onto a floured surface. Sprinkle with flour. Gently knead and add more flour as necessary, until the dough is no longer sticky.

Roll out to a rectangle ½ inches thick. Brush top with cooking oil and brush oil on the wheel of a pizza cutter. Use it to cut the dough in one inch squares. Repeat with scraps.

Place on a baking sheet prepared with nonstick baking spray or a baking mat. Bake in a preheated 450° oven for 15 minutes or until crispy and brown.

Cornish Game Hens

with Cornbread, Biscuit, and Giblet Dressing

Yield: 2 game hens, either 2 or 4 servings

Preheat oven to 450°.

Brining pork and chicken adds a world of flavor and moisture to the meat. I grabbed navel oranges off our tree and made up a brine for these game hens, which resulted in a bird that was fittin' to eat. We love giblets—all those things that come in that little bag inside poultry. I use them for giblet gravy and always include them in chicken and rice. They were simmered till tender, diced, and put in the dressing for this recipe.

2 (1½–2 pounds) Cornish Game Hens

Brine:

¼ cup kosher salt
5 cups water, divided
1 cup orange juice

4 sage leaves, crushed
2 bay leaves
10 peppercorns

Dressing:

3 cornmeal biscuits (about 2 cups), diced and toasted (see recipe, page 33)
1 stalk celery, finely diced
½ sweet onion, finely diced
1 tablespoon finely chopped sage leaves
Cooked giblets★
½ cup stock
½ teaspoon ground black pepper

★Remove giblet meat from neckbone. Mince along with the organ meats.

For Brine:

In a large pitcher, dissolve salt in 1 cup of warm water. Add remaining ingredients and stir well.

Wash hens. Remove giblet bag. Set aside.

Add hens to 1-gallon storage bag. Pour brine into bag and seal. Store in refrigerator. Brine for at least 8 hours. The hens can stay in the brine solution overnight.

Giblets and stock:

Place giblets in a small saucepan and cover with water. Add ½ teaspoon kosher salt and 2 fresh sage leaves. Cover and simmer for one hour or until tender. Set aside.

For dressing:

First, toast the biscuits. To toast, place in a single layer on a sheet pan or skillet. Heat oven to 450°. Cook until toasted.

Mix all ingredients in a small bowl. Add more stock if necessary to make dressing moist.

To assemble:

Preheat oven to 450°.

Rub hens with olive oil. Stuff the cavity of each bird with half the dressing. Place breast side up in a large cast-iron skillet. Roast at 450° for 1 hour or until the internal temperature of the thighs reached 165°. Remove from oven, tent with foil and let rest for 10 minutes before serving.

A whole bird may be used as one serving. For two servings, split the bird in half lengthwise.

Breakfast Garden Skillet
with Biscuit Crust

Yield: 3 servings

Preheat oven to 450°

Early on a Saturday morning, I noticed arugula and jalapeño peppers in my garden were ready. I didn't have enough arugula for a salad, just the right amount for a pizza topping. Arugula's peppery flavor is a nice substitution for sweet peppers. This pizza can be made using one skillet if you caramelize the onions in advance and give the skillet a chance to cool down before placing the crust. It's important to seed the tomatoes and get out as much water as possible to keep the crust from getting soggy. A biscuit crust pizza is made for baked eggs. The crust and the eggs take the same amount of time to cook.

1 medium sweet onion, thinly sliced
1 jalapeño pepper, diced
1 tablespoon bacon drippings
1 cup soft wheat self-rising flour
¼ cup unsalted butter, cubed and chilled

½ cup buttermilk
1 cup grated sharp cheddar cheese
1 tomato, halved, seeded and thinly sliced
1 cup arugula, washed well and dried
3 eggs

In a 9-inch cast-iron skillet, melt the bacon drippings over medium heat. Add onions and jalapeño pepper. Sauté for 10 to 15 minutes or until the onions have browned. Remove onions and pepper from skillet and set aside.

Wipe out skillet and let it cool.

In a medium bowl, add flour and butter. Rub or cut in until the flour resembles coarse meal. Stir in buttermilk until the flour is wet and forms a ball.

Make sure the skillet has a light coating of fat. Place the ball of dough in the skillet. Coat your fingers well with shortening or oil. Spread the dough evenly over the bottom and sides of skillet.

Sprinkle cheese evenly over crust. Top with onion/pepper mixture. Lightly tear arugula and spread over onion mixture.

Make a small well in the toppings for each of the three eggs. Crack an egg into a cup and gently pour into one of the wells. Repeat with the remaining eggs.

Bake at 450° until the crust is browned and the eggs are set to your degree of doneness.

Sprinkle with salt and pepper before serving.

Breakfast Garden Skillet

Hamburger Pot Pie
with Herb Biscuit Topper

Yield: 8 to 10 servings

Preheat oven to 350°

Ground beef and vegetables cook in a light gravy topped with savory biscuits to make a family pleasing dinner.

Filling:

2 cups potatoes in ½-inch cubes
2 cups carrots, peeled, in ½-inch cubes
1–2 tablespoons cooking oil
2 sweet onions, diced
2 celery stalks, diced
3 garlic cloves, diced

3 pounds ground chuck
3 tablespoons all-purpose flour
1 quart beef stock
½ cup tomato sauce
1 teaspoon kosher salt
½ teaspoon pepper

Herb biscuits:

2 cups self-rising flour
½ cup unsalted butter, cubed and chilled
1 tablespoon fresh thyme, chopped

2 tablespoon flat leaf parsley, chopped
1 cup buttermilk

For the filling:

Parboil potatoes and carrots for 5 minutes or until slightly tender. Drain and set aside.

Heat oil on medium high in a large kettle or skillet. Add onions and celery. Cook five minutes. Add garlic, cook two additional minutes.

Add ground beef to onion mixture. Cook until pink is gone, breaking up ground beef as it cooks.

Stir in flour. Cook, stirring constantly, until all the white has disappeared. Slowly stir in beef stock, stirring constantly. Add tomato sauce. Cook until mixture thickens. Add salt and pepper. Taste and adjust seasoning if necessary.

Pour mixture into a well-greased 3-quart casserole. Mix in potatoes and carrots.

For the herb biscuits:

Add flour to large bowl. Rub in butter until flour resembles coarse meal. Stir in herbs.

Pour in milk and stir until incorporated. Dough will be soft and sticky. Turn dough onto a well-floured surface. Sprinkle with flour and continue to work it in until dough is no longer sticky and holds its shape. Roll out to ½ inches thick. Cut biscuits with 2½-inch cutter dipped in flour. Repeat with remaining dough.

Cover meat mixture with biscuits. Brush tops with oil and sprinkle with salt and fresh ground pepper.

Bake at 350° for 40 minutes or until mixture is bubbly and biscuits are browned.

Skillet Pepperoni Pizza
with Biscuit Crust

Yield: 1 (12-inch) pizza

Preheat oven to 450°

Pizza was a lunchroom favorite during my school years. The lunchroom ladies made yeast dough topped with a seasoned meat sauce and then covered in cheddar cheese. Before take-out pizza shops were all the rage, the choices for eating pizza at home were to make a scratch pizza or purchase a store-bought pizza kit that had small jar of sauce, grated parmesan cheese, and the makings of dough. Now-a-days, any flavor pizza your heart desires is but a phone call away. I made this pizza today with my grandchildren. Take-out pizza can't hold a candle to the pleasure of cooking with kids in the kitchen, especially when the kids call you Nana. The red daisy in the photo was picked by my little Ella as soon as she got to my house today. You don't get that with pizza delivery.

Dough:

2 cups self-rising flour
1 teaspoon dried Italian seasoning
1 teaspoon garlic powder

4 tablespoons unsalted butter
1 cup buttermilk
Olive oil

Sauce:

½ cup pizza sauce

Toppings:

2 cups grated mozzarella cheese
3 to 4 ounces pepperoni slices
Grated Parmesan cheese

To make the dough:

Place flour, Italian seasoning, and garlic powder in a bowl. Stir with hand. Cut or rub in butter until flour resembles coarse meal. Add buttermilk and stir until dough is wet. Turn out onto a floured surface. Sprinkle dough with flour. Gently knead, adding more flour as needed, until dough is no longer sticky.

Coat a 12-inch cast-iron skillet with olive oil. Place dough in skillet and sprinkle with olive oil. Press dough evenly over bottom of skillet and partially up the side. Stick several times with the tines of a fork. Bake in a preheated 450° oven for 5 minutes.

To assemble:

Spread pizza sauce over dough. Top with mozzarella cheese. Add pepperoni on top of cheese.

Bake in a preheated 450° oven for 15 minutes, or until edges of crust are brown and cheese has melted.

Sprinkle with Parmesan cheese before eating.

Double-crusted Summer Vegetable Pie

Yield: 1 (12-inch) pie

Preheat oven to 350°

Our summer Southern vegetables are heavenly. The filling in this pie contains four of my favorites: tomatoes, okra, butterbeans, and corn. There's an ongoing debate about butterbeans versus lima beans. The tiny green limas are butterbeans to me. Always have been, always will be. My favorite variety of corn is called Silver Queen. A brand called Today's Harvest carries both frozen butterbeans (tiny green limas) and Silver Queen corn. Their products are high quality and I've never been disappointed. This savory pie reminds me of vegetable soup in a crust. I use the skillet to cook the bacon and filling, then pour the filling into a bowl while I prepare the crust in the same skillet. Getting by with only two dirty vessels for a complete meal is a big score.

Vegetable filling:

4 pieces bacon, cooked crisp and drippings reserved
1 medium sweet onion, diced
2 cups butterbeans
2 cups cut fresh or frozen okra
¼ cup all-purpose flour

1 (14.5-ounce) can diced tomatoes
2 cups Silver Queen frozen or fresh cut corn
2 cups chicken stock
Salt and pepper to taste

Biscuit crust:

2 cups self-rising soft winter wheat flour
½ cup unsalted butter, cubed and chilled
1½ cups grated sharp cheddar cheese

1 teaspoon garlic powder
2 tablespoons finely chopped parsley
1 cup buttermilk

For vegetable filling:

While skillet is still hot from cooking the bacon, add onion, butterbeans, and okra. Cook 15 to 20 minutes on medium heat until vegetables are soft.

Stir in flour. Cook and stir until all the white from the flour is gone.

Add in tomatoes, with their juice, corn, and chicken stock. Stir well.

Crumble bacon and stir into filling.

Bring back to a simmer and cook, stirring occasionally, until mixture thickens.

Taste for seasoning and adjust.

Pour filling into a large bowl. Clean skillet to prepare for making the crust.

For biscuit crust:

Place flour in a large bowl. Rub or cut in butter until flour resembles coarse meal.

Using hands, stir in cheese, garlic powder, and parsley.

Make a well in the flour and pour in buttermilk. Stir with a spoon until the dough is wet.

Turn out onto a well-floured surface. Sprinkle flour on dough. Gently knead and add flour, as needed, until dough is no longer sticky and holds its shape.

Prepare skillet by coating insides with a thin layer of bacon drippings or solid vegetable shortening.

Divide the dough into two pieces. Make one piece a little larger than the other. You need about a 60 to 40 ratio.

Using your fingers and hands, press the larger piece evenly along the bottom and sides of the greased skillet. If the dough is sticky, sprinkle with a little more flour. Greasing your fingers helps, too.

Once the bottom and sides of the skillet are evenly covered with the dough, pour in vegetable filling.

Take remaining piece of dough and roll out to a circle approximately 12 inches in diameter. Transfer the dough to the skillet. I find the transfer is easier if I roll the dough around my rolling pin and then unroll it on top of the filling. Fit the dough on top. If some overlaps, cut it off and use it to patch empty spaces, if needed. If you do need to patch it, simply pat the seams with a wet finger.

Brush top crust with vegetable oil or bacon drippings. Cut a few slits in the top for venting.

Place in a 350° preheated oven for 40 minutes or until the crust is golden brown and the filling is bubbly.

Remove from oven and let sit for 5 minutes before serving.

Double-crusted Summer Vegetable Pie

Barbecue Pork on Mashed Potato Biscuit

with Cajun Crispy Fried Onions

Yield: 4 servings

If you're not aware that Southerners are passionate about barbecue, then you haven't talked to many Southerners. We love it better than we love our luggage. There are significant regional differences in barbecue sauce preferences, too: South Carolina has mustard-based, North Carolina has vinegar-based, and north Alabama has white mayonnaise–based. Peppered throughout the South is smoky and sweet sauce, which is my favorite. You should know that we consider barbecue a noun, not a verb. Barbecue is what we eat; we don't barbecue our meat. We cook our meat in a particular manner and add certain kinds of sauces, which turns into barbecue. There's spelling variations: barbecue, barbeque, and BBQ. Folks don't seem to be quite as picky about the spelling as they are other aspects of barbecue. We eat lots of barbecue and relish every bite.

Leftover barbecue chicken, pork, or beef can be used to make a sandwich on mashed potato biscuits topped with fried onions.

4 mashed potato biscuits split open (see recipe, page 51)
Leftover barbecue meat, shredded
Barbecue sauce (use your favorite homemade or commercially prepared)
Cajun Crispy Fried Onions (recipe on following page)

Place two biscuit halves on a plate for one serving. Top with meat and drizzle on sauce. Add fried onions on the top. Serve with coleslaw on the side.

Cajun Crispy Fried Onions

Preheat oil to 350°

1 medium sweet onion, thinly sliced
1 tablespoon buttermilk
1 tablespoon Cajun seasoning
½ cup all-purpose flour
Cooking oil

Add sliced onions and buttermilk to a gallon plastic re-sealable bag. Mix until buttermilk has coated all the onions.

Mix seasoning and flour in a small bowl. Pour into bag with onions; shake until all the onions are coated.

In batches, drop breaded onions in oil that has been heated to 350°. Fry for three to four minutes, stirring frequently, or until golden brown. Drain on paper towel. Season with salt, if desired, while the onions are still hot.

Barbecue Pork on Mashed Potato Biscuit

Grilled Salad

with Biscuit Croutons

Yield: 2 servings

Leftover biscuits have many uses. I threw these on the grill and made croutons for our salad. If you've never tried charred Romaine lettuce, you've missed something unbelievably good. It makes me laugh to think what my grandparents would say about eating burned lettuce! This makes a wonderful vegetarian meal, or you can make the salad along with your favorite grilled meat or fish. Timing is critically important for this meal to come out right, especially if you're cooking meat. It's best to cook the meat, remove it from the grill, and tent it to keep warm while the vegetables are cooking. We cooked sirloin steak by marinating it in Dale's Steak Seasoning for one hour at room temperature. We grilled over medium-high heat for three minutes and flip after every three minutes for a total cook time of twelve minutes. Brush the vegetables with olive oil and season with your favorite seasoning. I use a blend of four parts kosher salt to one part ground black pepper to one part garlic powder.

2 ears corn
1 medium sweet onion, sliced ½ inches thick
6–8 cherry-type tomatoes, skewered
2 leftover biscuits, split in half
2 heads romaine lettuce, remove any damaged or yellowed outer leaves
Olive oil
Salt and pepper or your favorite seasoning blend
Blue cheese sprinkles, optional

Brush corn, onion slices, and tomatoes with olive oil. Sprinkle with seasoning. Set aside.

Drizzle romaine lettuce with olive oil and sprinkle with seasoning and set aside.

Place corn and onion slices on a hot grill. Each will take about 12 minutes cook time. Rotate the corn as each side gets grill marks. Flip the onion when it gets grill marks. Remove to a platter when done.

Brush the insides of the split biscuits with olive oil. Sprinkle with seasoning.

Place the tomatoes and biscuits on the grill. Flip the tomatoes as soon as they blister and start to char. Watch the biscuits carefully and turn once they brown. Remove to a platter.

The lettuce is charred last because it takes a small amount of time and needs to be eaten immediately. Place it on the grill and flip it as soon as it's charred. The lettuce cooks in about 3 to 5 minutes.

Assemble the salad on your plate. Drizzle the romaine with your favorite dressing or vinaigrette, if you'd like. I don't find that it needs additional dressing. I like to cut the corn from the cob but leave the rest of the vegetables whole.

Cut each biscuit half in four pieces and place on top of salad.

Chicken 'n Dumplins

A few generations back, when backyard chickens were more the rule than the exception, chickens were kept more for egg production than for meat. Young chickens lay eggs and have the tenderest meat. As a chicken ages, the meat toughens and the egg-laying capacity lessens until the old hen "jes' cain't lay no mo'." A young tender chicken, called a fryer, only has one chicken dinner to offer, but dozens of eggs. It follows, logically, that Southerners, especially poor ones in the rural parts of the South, didn't eat fried chicken every day. It was saved for a special occasion such as Sunday Dinner, especially if the preacher was coming.

As hens aged and stopped producing eggs, they were no longer valuable and, in fact, became a liability. They still had to be fed but gave nothing in return. For poor people who could barely scrape by and keep themselves fed, a hen that stopped contributing would soon find itself in a cook pot.

Because the old hens had tough meat, they were simmered and stewed for a long period of time until the meat tenderized. A stewed hen could be eaten just as it was and feed a fair number of people. Somewhere along the line, the idea of stretching the meal but adding dumplings came along. Southerners didn't create dumplings. All cuisines have a form of dumplings known by familiar names such as gnocchi and wontons. Even ravioli is a form of a stuffed dumpling. The addition of dumplings to the pot of stewed chicken created an inexpensive meal that fed a lot of people. Delicious, nutritious, simple, and practical: the hallmark of Southern cuisine. Folks, who often went without sufficient food, got much-needed protein and lots of carbohydrates to fuel them for their high level of daily activity and back-breaking work. Chicken and dumplings were born out of necessity and practicality.

My history with chicken and dumplings is spotted and ranges from wonderful childhood memories to personal kitchen failures to shortcut methods to eventual success with scratch dumplings. Chicken and dumplings often graced my grandmother's holiday table. Her dumplings always had perfect texture: toothsome but not tough, tender but yet firm enough to hold up in boiling liquid. As a child, I was allowed to pull up a chair to the stove and drop dumplings into a pot of boiling liquid.

Many years later, as a young bride, I thought it fitting that I recreate this favorite dish for my Southern husband. Certainly, the training in my grandmother's kitchen was sufficient and I didn't feel the need to consult my grandmother or a cookbook. Stewing chicken was easy and I had done that many times. Now, it was time for me to add dumplings to the pot. What resulted was a big pot of chicken and dumpling. Not dumplings, just one big dumpling. I queried the chief dumpling maker, my grandmother, and her advice to me was surprising.

She said, "Shug, jes' git you a package of them flour tortillers (tortillas). Cut 'em up with a keen knife, jes' like you would dumplings. They's jes as good and way yonder easier than a–tryin' to make scratch dumplings."

Granny had come to the point in her life that she was enamored with kitchen shortcuts. Many convenient foods had become available and she was getting "flat-out tired of standing on her feet to cook all the time."

Her flour "tortiller" method worked, and I didn't give scratch dumplings another thought until a few years after I started writing my Southern food blog. I professed to be a Southern food champion, but felt somewhat dishonest about the proclamation since I didn't know a hill of beans about making the Southern iconic dish: chicken and dumplings. I wanted to poll my reading audience to determine what dish they would like to see me write about that wasn't included in my ever-increasing index of Southern foods. I felt I should offer four choices and one was chicken and dumplings. Before I posted the poll, I talked myself out of it.

What if chicken and dumplings wins? How on Earth will I explain that I'm a fake and can only make chicken and dumplings using tortillers?

So, that option was eliminated just to be safe. Again, before I posted the poll, I had another conversation with myself.

You should keep chicken and dumplings in the poll. If that's what your readers, who are so sweet, kind, and supportive, really want to see, you've got to figure out how to make them.

The poll, including chicken and dumplings, was posted, giving readers the option of four dishes they wished I would prepare and write about. Not only did chicken and dumplings win the poll, but it won by a landslide. I was now in a fine mess. Granny had passed away long before, so I couldn't go to her for help. There wasn't anyone else who I knew to be a dumpling expert. The best I could do was to read everything I could find about authentic Southern chicken and dumplings. As I studied and researched, I had an epiphany, and the part of Granny's kitchen instructions that had been stuck in an irretrievable portion of my memory bank rose to the surface: "Shug, ya got to drop them dumplings in the eye of the boil. The eye of boil is what's keeping them held together."

That was it! I hadn't been getting the stock up to a full, rolling boil before dropping them. I didn't have an eye of the boil. My dumplings were waterlogged and dissolving in the stock. I eagerly gathered all my ingredients, along with my newfound knowledge of an old memory, and set out to make chicken and dumplings.

As soon as the stewed chicken was cooked and removed from the stock, I cranked the heat under the stockpot up to high and waited like a child for Christmas morning. Pushing aside the axiom "a watched pot never boils," I didn't take my eyes off the stock, eagerly awaiting the arrival of the eye. And, arrive it did. A full, rolling boil created an eye that was a beautiful sight to behold. Dropping the dumplings in, one by one, I held my breath to see if they would hold their shape. And they did. This masterpiece will be a pot of chicken and dumplings, not a pot of chicken and dumpling. My exuberance was dampened by the fact that I couldn't call Granny and share the good news. I just looked to the heavens and could feel her smiling down on me.

Chicken and Dumplings

Yield: approximately 1 gallon

 Authentic Southern Chicken and Dumplings is time-consuming, although there's nothing complicated about the recipe. To get an authentic flavor, a whole chicken should be stewed for a couple hours. This dish will only be as good as your stock and chicken. Slow simmering brings out the best flavor of the chicken and keeps the meat from being cooked to death. While the chicken is stewing, make dumplings and set them aside to dry. Once the chicken is sufficiently cooked until tender, remove it from the stockpot and cooled. As soon as it's cool enough to handle, all the meat is picked from the bone, shredded, and eventually put back in the stock along with dumplings. For the dumplings, I use my standard buttermilk biscuit recipe, roll out the dough thin and cut into strips.

Chicken and stock:

1 (4–5 pound) whole roasting chicken
4 carrots, washed and broken in half
3 celery stalks, washed and broken in half
1 sweet onion, cut in half

2 bay leaves
1 tablespoon kosher salt
1 teaspoon ground black pepper
12 cups water

Dumplings:

2 cups self-rising soft winter wheat flour
½ cup butter, cubed

1 cup buttermilk

For chicken and stock:

Wash chicken and place whole chicken and contents of giblet bag in a large stockpot with a colander insert.

There's no need to peel carrots and onions since the vegetables are only used to flavor the stock and will be removed before eating. Add carrots, celery, onion, bay leaves, salt, and pepper to stock pot.

Add water.

Cover and bring to a rapid boil. Reduce heat to simmer. Cook on a slow simmer for 2 hours or until the meat is falling-off-the-bone tender.

Remove colander and all the contents from stock. Set chicken aside to cool and discard the rest of the contents of the colander. Remove stock pot from heat. Keep covered.

As soon as chicken is cool enough to handle, pick all the meat from the bones, shred it, and set aside. Chop giblets in to small pieces. Discard skin, fat, and bones.

While the chicken is stewing, make dumplings and set aside to dry.

For dumplings:

Add flour to a large bowl and cut or rub in butter until flour resembles coarse meal. Stir in buttermilk and mix until dough is wet.

Turn onto a well-floured surface. Sprinkle flour on top. Knead gently, adding flour as necessary, until dough is no longer sticky.

Roll out to ½ inches thick. Cut in equal squares using a pizza cutter or sharp knife. Set aside on a floured baking sheet to dry.

After all the chicken meat has been picked off the bones and shredded, turn heat up to high understock pot and keep covered. Bring to a full, rolling boil.

Remove cover and drop four dumplings, one at the time, into the eye of the boil. Return lid for 15 to 20 seconds or until the full boil returns. Repeat until all dumplings have been dropped in the stock. Add chicken meat, one handful at the time, and cover after each addition to keep the temperature of the stock up. Stir slightly after all meat has been added.

Turn heat down to medium and cook for 20 to 25 minutes until dumplings are cooked through.

Biscuits and Toppings in Diners

Diners represent comfortable causal eating establishments that offer menus filled with familiar dishes that are as far from being mysterious and fussy as you can get. There's no need for waitstaff to explain the menu and ask you if you have any questions. You might need to know the options for the Blue Plate Special, Plate Lunch Special, or Meat and Three, but that's about as far as the explaining needs to go. Everything served reminds you of good eats from the kitchens of your mother, grandmother, and favorite aunt. There's no need for your palate to prepare for an unknown taste adventure. Cozy up to the counter or sit at a booth and relax as you enjoy simple favorites.

Choose your favorite biscuits to enjoy with the toppings included in this chapter. There's no right or wrong answer.

Sausage Gravy and Biscuits

Yield: 6 servings

Browned pork sausage in a milky sauce is one of the South's most popular dishes. I prefer sausage gravy, heavy on the sausage. Stretch the gravy further by increasing the amount of flour and milk. I prefer Jimmy Dean's Original or Sage sausage.

1 pound bulk sausage
cooking oil (optional)
¼ cup all-purpose flour
1½–2 cups milk
salt and pepper to taste

Brown 1 pound of bulk sausage in a cast-iron skillet. Don't drain.

Add flour and stir. Cook for about 3 minutes until all the white and lumps from the flour have disappeared.

Gradually add milk, stirring constantly. Add as much milk as you need to reach the desired consistency.

Make sure to scrape up all the "goodies" from the bottom of the pan as you stir. There's lots of flavor in the goodies.

Continue to cook and stir until the gravy thickens.

Serve immediately over biscuits.

Bacon Tomato Gravy

Yield: 4 to 6 servings

When you combine bacon, tomatoes, and onions, the result is sure to be fittin' to eat. Make gravy out of the ingredients and you become a superstar. Tomato gravy is as old as the hills. Generation after generation grew up loving it. Fresh or canned tomatoes can be used.

4 slices bacon
1 medium sweet onion, diced
2 tablespoons flour
1 (14.5 ounce) can diced tomatoes
2 cups milk
½ teaspoon kosher salt
½ teaspoon ground black pepper

Fry bacon in a cast-iron skillet over medium heat till crisp. Remove from pan and set aside. Reserve two tablespoons of the bacon drippings.

Sauté onion in bacon drippings over medium heat about 15 minutes or until onion is soft.

Add flour to skillet and stir well until flour and bacon grease have mixed. Continue cooking and stir occasionally until the flour mixture is the color of peanut butter. This may take 15 to 20 minutes.

Add tomatoes and stir well.

Slowly add milk, stir continuously until mixed. Simmer over medium heat until thickened. Add salt and pepper. Taste and adjust seasoning as needed. Garnish with crumbled bacon—or eat all the bacon yourself as a reward for the cook.

Tomato Gravy is especially good served over Bacon Cathead Biscuits (see recipe page 61).

Jelly and Butter

Good jelly is as much a treasure as a good biscuit. We have a small grape arbor in our backyard and we grow a Southern grape variety called muscadine. The flavor is unlike any other grape. Muscadines are deep purple and their cousins, scuppernongs, are golden. Southern children are taught how to take the grapes in their mouths and separate the hulls and seeds from the meat and juice using only tongues and teeth. The hulls and seeds are spit out and the meat and juice consumed. I never learned the proper way of eating muscadines and scuppernongs and always cheated by using my hands. The flavor is tart and slightly musky. Squirrels and birds start feasting on our grapes before their quite ready to harvest. Most years, they leave us just enough for a batch of jelly.

Muscadine Jelly

Yield: 3 to 4 half-pint jars

To extract juice, wash and pick over 2 gallons muscadine grapes. Place in a stockpot and cover with water. Bring to a boil and cook for 25 minutes, mashing with back of wooden spoon occasionally. I have my grandmother's potato masher that I use for this, but a wooden spoon works just fine. Remove all the grape pieces. Strain juice through a cheesecloth. Store in refrigerator overnight. Strain again before cooking.

4 cups muscadine juice, strained through a cheesecloth
1 (1.75-ounce) box powdered pectin
3 cups sugar

Wash canning jars in soapy water. Rinse and sterilize by boiling for 10 minutes. Keep hot until ready for use. Wash lids and rings and place in a small pot. Bring up to a boil and then let simmer until ready for use.

Mix juice and powdered pectin in a large pot and bring to a boil. Add sugar all at once, stirring until sugar dissolves. Boil rapidly until mixture reaches 220° (or 8° above boiling point if you're in high altitudes) or until the mixture coats the back of a metal spoon, about 20 to 30 minutes. Remove from heat and quickly skim off foam.

Pour jelly immediately into hot canning jars, leaving ¼-inch headspace. Wipe rims and adjust lids.

Process in a boiling water bath for 5 minutes.

Remove jars and set on a kitchen towel. Let them sit for 12 hours undisturbed.

A cane syrup bottle and a gallon jug used to sell cane juice.

Cane Syrup

Sugar cane thrives in humid and hot climates. That pretty much describes anywhere in the Deep South. During my childhood, it was common to see sugar cane fields in southeastern Alabama. It wasn't grown for sugar, but rather for chewing or syrup making.

Granddaddy loved to bring home canes for us. He'd remove his little keen knife from his pocket, cut a section off the large cane, peel it, and then cut the inside part into chunks for us to chew. The juice of sugar cane is bold and daring. I had an aversion to the texture, so enjoying a "chew" was left for someone else.

Just down the street from my grandparent's home, a mule driven cane press operated during harvest time. Harnessed to the press, the mule walked around in a circle while the press extracted juice from the sugar cane. There was always a big cast-iron pot full of juice bubbling away and converting the cane juice to cane syrup. The cane press operator sold both the juice and the syrup.

During the simple times of my childhood, a trip to the cane press held all the excitement of Disney World. The heavy perfume of cane syrup hung in the air. People gathered around to watch the mule work. Farmers in their denim overalls inspected the canes and chose the best ones to share with children just like granddaddy shared with us. Gallons of cane juice were on display in clear jugs. Cane syrup was packed up in tin cans. It's a shame that so many of today's children can't appreciate the excitement found in events that aren't dependent on technology.

Cane syrup's flavor is more akin to molasses or sorghum syrup than to maple syrup. In fact, cane syrup and maple syrup are so different, it's hard to believe they have anything in common. The flavor of maple syrup is dainty compared to the boldness of cane syrup.

Cane Syrup and Peanut Butter

The combination of cane syrup and peanut butter is unbelievably good. This mixture is good on waffles and pancakes, also.

2 tablespoons peanut butter
1 tablespoon cane syrup

Mix well. Spread on biscuits.

Cane Syrup and Butter

Cane syrup mixed with softened butter is made for sopping. The ratio of syrup to butter is a matter of personal preference. My granddaddy had cane syrup and biscuits for breakfast every day of his life. His favorite brand of store-bought cane syrup was Top o' the World. The company that produced that brand has been out of business for a long time. Today, I use Steen's Cane Syrup.

1 tablespoon cane syrup
1 tablespoon soften butter

Pour syrup onto small plate. Mix in soften butter with a fork. Break off small pieces of biscuit and sop up the syrup.

Cane Syrup Filled Biscuit

Southern children learn to eat biscuits filled with syrup. It's a childhood ritual.

1 biscuit
Small amount of cane syrup

Make a hole partially through a biscuit using your finger. Fill hole with cane syrup. Hand the biscuit to a happy child.

Chocolate Gravy

Yield: 8 to 10 servings

My friend, Dawn Wagner, told me that one of her favorite childhood memories was the Chocolate Gravy her Mama would make on Saturdays to top their biscuits. On one of the days Dawn came to my kitchen to help me, I thought it would be a nice gesture to make Chocolate Gravy. The day wasn't Saturday and I'm not Mama, but I sent her home with a container of Chocolate Gravy and a fresh batch of Buttermilk Biscuits.

4 tablespoons unsalted butter

⅔ cup granulated sugar

2 tablespoons all-purpose flour

⅓ cup cocoa powder

2 cups half-and-half or whole milk

Melt butter in a cast-iron skillet. Add sugar, flour, and cocoa. Stir until sugar is dissolved and all ingredients are well mixed.

Remove from heat and slowly whisk in half of the half-and-half stirring constantly to prevent lumps.

Return to heat and add remaining half-and-half, whisking constantly. Continue whisking and cooking until gravy has thickened.

Serve immediately with Buttermilk Biscuits.

Compound Butters

Compounds butters are wonderful for entertaining. The name compound *makes them sound much more complicated than they are; they're softened butter with stuff mixed in. People are generally impressed and have no idea how utterly simple they are to make. I like to have compound butters, sweet or savory, for house guests. They add such a beautiful touch and make your guests feel special. An added bonus is deliciousness. Peach and strawberry butters are heavenly on a hot biscuit of your choice. Store them in a covered glass jar and bring to room temperature before serving. Or, place the soft whipped butter on waxed paper and roll into a log. Chill well and slice off the desired amounts for each serving. Rewrap with waxed paper and store in the refrigerator.*

Peach Butter

½ cup softened unsalted butter

4 tablespoons peach preserves

¼ teaspoon ginger

¼ teaspoon cinnamon

Whip with an electric mixer until soft.

Strawberry Butter

½ cup softened unsalted butter

2 tablespoons strawberry jam

1 teaspoon vanilla

Whip with an electric mixer until smooth.

Along with the little white bowl, amaryllis lilies that were pass-a-longs from my grandmother, are priceless.

The Little White Bowl

The earliest memory of breakfast at my grandparent's kitchen table contains a little white pottery bowl. It was always there, right next to a bottle of cane syrup and a dish of softened butter. The importance of the little bowl was lost on me as a child. Back then, it was just a bowl. Today, it's my priceless treasure.

Sitting atop a black and white speckled enamel table, the little white bowl was filled with redeye gravy made from fried ham and coffee and was on the table each time breakfast was served. Granny didn't fry ham every day. When she did, she made an ample supply of redeye gravy; much more than could be consumed over several days of breakfast. She'd refrigerate the leftover gravy and reheat it every morning. When the gravy supply got low, that was her signal to fry more ham. The gravy that was left became the starter for a new batch.

I use the little white bowl infrequently. The tiny cracks in the finish make me scared to death to handle it much for fear that it will break. Filled with blue mophead hydrangea blossoms, it makes a lovely centerpiece for a breakfast table, but I've stopped using it for that purpose, too.

A stamp on the bottom of the 5-inch by 3-inch bowl that reads U. S. A. is the only identifiable mark on the bowl. Cracks are on the surface and scuff marks are on the inside and outside. The patina has turned from white to cream. The average person would say the bowl isn't spectacular looking and not even worthy of inclusion in a yard sale. That same average person wouldn't know the hands of my grandparents touched the little white bowl countless times. As far as I'm concerned, anything my grandparents touched turned to gold.

Country Ham and Redeye Gravy

Yield: 3 to 4 servings

Country ham is salt cured with a process that takes months to complete. Benson's Country Hams is one of the few sources left for hams cured the old-fashioned way. Redeye gravy is made in the pan after country ham's been fried. The gravy is thin and customarily served over grits. Place a few slices of fried ham on leftover biscuits and drizzle on redeye gravy. You must eat it with a fork and knife, but it turns day-old biscuits into something good. The biscuits hold up to the watery gravy better if they're toasted. Ham is lean and requires added fat to fry.

1 pound country ham, sliced thin and in 3-in by 2-in pieces
1 tablespoon bacon drippings
½ cup strong brewed black coffee
2 cups water
1 teaspoon honey

Place bacon drippings in a 9-inch cast-iron skillet over medium heat. After the bacon drippings melt, add the ham in batches and cook until browned on both sides. Remove to a platter and set aside.

Add coffee to skillet and use a wooden spoon to scrape up all the bits from the bottom. Add water and honey, stir.

Place browned ham slices back in skillet. Continue to cook on medium heat until the gravy is reduced by one-third.

Slice open leftover biscuits. Place several slices of ham on each side of the biscuits. Drizzle gravy over ham.

Biscuit Neighbors and Kin

With a few simple modifications, basic biscuit dough is easily transformed into something that doesn't resemble modern biscuits. Hopefully, this chapter will encourage experimentation with biscuits and instill confidence that knowing basic biscuit techniques will lead to wonderful homemade recipes. In the South, we loosely define relatives to include people close to the family not related by blood. Customarily, children are taught to call special adult friends of the family Aunt and Uncle. We consider it ill-mannered for a child to call an adult by their first name, yet it seems impersonal for close family friends to be called Mr. and Mrs. So, it's logical to include recipes that are closely related to biscuits in a biscuit cookbook. We don't want to leave anyone out.

Hound dogs are as much a part of Southern tradition as grits. Meet our magnificent Basset Hound, Belle.

Hush, Puppy!

According to folklore, this traditional Southern dish got its name when hunters mixed up a similar concoction to feed to their barking hunting hounds, telling them, "Hush, puppy!" Traditional hushpuppies contain green onions. Whether they were included in the mixture fed to hush the barking dogs is left to your imagination. Nothing can be found in literature to confirm or deny the absence or presence of onions. Hushpuppies are a standard fried fish accompaniment. My grandmother would use the breading left over from fish to make hushpuppy batter. That's another fine example of efficient Southern cooking.

Hushpuppies

Yield: 30 pieces

Preheat 3 inches of cooking oil to 350°

Tiny balls of cornmeal dough flavored with green onions are deep fried to make a perfect match for fried fish. If you've ever had hushpuppies that were greasy and soggy, I'm just as sorry as I can be. They shouldn't be greasy at all if the proper cooking technique is followed. You need a cooking thermometer to maintain the proper temperature.

1 cup stone ground cornmeal (not cornbread mix)
½ cup all-purpose soft winter wheat flour
½ teaspoon salt
½ teaspoon baking powder
1½ tablespoons sugar
¼ cup green onions, finely diced
1 cup buttermilk
1 egg

Add first 5 ingredients to a bowl and stir well. Stir in green onions.

In a separate bowl, whisk together buttermilk and egg. Add to flour mixture and stir well.

Heat 3 inches of cooking oil to 350° in a pan.

Drop teaspoons of batter into the hot oil. About one minute after one side starts to brown, flip to the other side using a large slotted spoon. Turn occasionally and don't let one side get a lot browner than the other or the hushpuppies will be hard to flip over. They will want to stay with the light side up. If this happens, turn the light side down and submerge them in the grease using the slotted spoon to hold them down. Fry in batches and don't overcrowd the pan. Keep an eye on the temperature of the oil and be sure to keep it at 350°. Each batch will take 5 to 7 minutes to cook. Take them up when they are a deep golden brown.

Drain on a rack. Sprinkle with additional kosher salt while still hot. Serve with cocktail sauce.

Cocktail Sauce

⅓ cup ketchup
¼ cup chili sauce
Juice of ½ of a lemon
1 teaspoon horseradish
1–2 teaspoons of honey

Mix all ingredients together.

Hushpuppies

Cheese Wafers

Yield: approximately 90 (1-inch) wafers

Preheat oven to 375°

    Delicate enough for a tea party yet sturdy enough for a cocktail party, cheese wafers and cheese straws have shown up at more Southern food–related events than Carter's has liver pills. For cheese straws, place the dough in a cookie press and make ribbons of dough on the baking sheet. The shape of cheese wafers more closely resembles its biscuit cousin, historical biscuits, than do cheese straws. Historical biscuits were made without leavening, which resulted in a flat, crisp disk.

8 ounces sharp cheddar cheese, grated while cold and brought to room temperature
½ cup unsalted butter, room temperature
1½ all-purpose flour
½ teaspoon kosher salt
¼ teaspoon cayenne pepper, or to taste
½ teaspoon dry mustard
1 tablespoon water, optional

Cream cheddar cheese and butter with an electric mixer until smooth. Mix together flour, salt, cayenne pepper, and dry mustard. Gradually add to cheese mixture and mix on low speed until incorporated. Add water if dough is too dry to stick together. The dough should be soft and dense.

Divide the dough in half and roll each half into two cylinders about 1 inch thick. Each cylinder will be about 16 inches. Wrap in waxed paper and chill in refrigerator for at least one hour.

Cut into ¼-inch slices. Place slices 1 inch apart on a baking sheet sprayed with nonstick spray.

Bake in a 375° preheated oven for about 18 minutes, or until edges are slightly brown. Baking sheets may need to be rotated during baking.

Remove from oven. Use a spatula to gently coax the wafers from the baking sheet and transfer wafers to a cooling rack. Cool completely. Store at room temperature in an airtight container and place waxed paper or parchment paper between layers.

Irish Soda Bread

Yield: 1 loaf

Preheat oven to 425°

The traditional version of this bread is rustic and meant to be simple, just like biscuits. It has a hard crust and sounds hollow when tapped.

It's essentially biscuit dough without adding additional fat except what's in the buttermilk, and the dough is shaped into a loaf instead of small individual portions. There are many Americanized versions floating around, but the traditional version used but four ingredients: all-purpose flour, soda, salt, and buttermilk. This version uses whole wheat flour, in additional to white, and produces a darker, more flavorful bread. Folk lore has it that you cut an X to get the devil out and a cross if the bread is to be blessed. You need to make a decision about your personal situation.

3 cups buttermilk
1½ teaspoons baking soda
4 cups stone ground whole wheat flour

2 cups all-purpose soft winter wheat flour
2 teaspoons kosher salt

Stir baking soda into buttermilk and set aside. If the mixture bubbles, the baking soda is still good. If it doesn't bubble, you need to buy more.

Place both types of flour and salt in a large mixing bowl and stir.

Make a well in the center and pour in buttermilk and soda. Stir until the flour is wet.

Turn out onto a floured surface. Sprinkle with flour. Knead gently and add more flour as necessary until the dough is no longer sticky. Form into a ball and place on baking sheet sprayed with nonstick spray or covered with a baking mat.

Using hands, press out the dough in a circle that is 1½ inches thick.

Using a sharp knife, make an X ¼-inch deep in the top of the dough. Lightly brush top with cooking oil.

Bake in a preheated 425° oven for 25 minutes; reduce heat to 350° for an additional 15 minutes.

Cool on a baking rack. For best results, the loaf shouldn't be cut for 6 hours. Best of luck trying to wait that long.

Spinach Parmesan Scones

Yield: 16 scones

Preheat oven to 450°

Scones and biscuits are either similar or different according to who you ask. Some think scones are sweet and usually have add-ins such as fruit or nuts. I have a chapter in this book devoted to dessert biscuits, so the sweet versus savory argument doesn't pass muster with me. The biggest difference supported by literature is the addition of egg to the scone batter. I took the egg principle, added it to a biscuit batter with the addition of savory elements. The outcome is quite nice, if I do say so. Serve warm for best results.

2 cups self-rising soft winter wheat flour
½ cup unsalted butter, cubed and chilled
1 cup grated parmesan cheese
10-ounce package frozen chopped spinach, thawed and excess water removed
½ cup buttermilk
1 egg

Add flour to bowl. Rub or cut in butter until flour resembles coarse meal. Stir in parmesan cheese and spinach.

Whisk egg into buttermilk and pour into flour mixture, Stir until flour is wet.

Turn out onto a floured surface. Sprinkle with flour and knead gently, add more flour as needed until dough is no longer sticky.

Shape dough into a rectangle 1-inch thick. Cut in eight equal squares and cut each square diagonally.

Place 1 inch apart on a baking sheet sprayed with a nonstick spray or covered with a baking mat. Brush tops with cooking oil.

Bake in a preheated 450° oven for 17 to 20 minutes or until golden brown. Serve warm.

Found at an antique shop, these glasses are exactly like the glasses Granny used to cut out tea cakes.

Granny's Tea Cakes

It's hard to describe the taste of a Southern Tea Cake: not as sweet as a sugar cookie but sweeter than a biscuit. If you want sugar cookies, make sugar cookies. But, don't make a batch of Southern Tea Cakes and declare, "These are the worst sugar cookies I've ever eaten."

Shug, these ain't sugar cookies.

Authentic Southern Tea Cakes are made from ingredients that even poor Southerners were likely to have on hand: flour, sugar, butter, eggs, and buttermilk. Spices were not always affordable; extracts or flavorings were a tad bit more accessible.

My grandmother's recipe is the only one I've seen that directs you to mix wet and dry ingredients together at the start. I would love to know the story behind that. This recipe was handed down from my grandmother's mother, and I don't know the first experimenter to test the mixing technique. I caution you to pulse the ingredients until the flour is wet or it will fly out of the bowl and all over your kitchen.

This little tea cake has special meaning for me. It's the only thing resembling a cookie that I ever knew my grandmother to bake. Outside of cobblers and occasional pies, she wasn't a big baker. She preferred cooking over baking. I follow right along in those footsteps, too, but I do remember her making these tea cakes. If I was with her when she made them, she'd give me the job of cutting them out with a vintage juice glass that had beautiful designs of oranges and leaves. She never owned a cookie cutter and considered them extravagant. If she wanted to make big biscuits or cookies and a juice glass was too small, she used a soup can or a Vienna sausage can.

We would cut out the tea cakes and bake them. Then, we'd remove them from the oven, cool slightly, stack them high on a plain dinner plate from the cupboard, and set the plate in the middle of the enamel kitchen table. We sat down to the table together. Granny sat across from me, wearing a flower-printed house dress and assumed her usual 45° angle in her chair. She never sat perpendicular to the table, always at an angle. She'd rest her left arm on the back of her chair, pick up a tea cake in her right, and tell me the story of how her mother used to make these very same tea cakes for her and her siblings.

No matter how many times she told the story, she always interjected, "And we was some young'uns who was mighty proud to get 'em."

Despite my youth, I knew these tea cakes were special to my grandmother. She grew up in the poorest part of the Deep South and treats were few and far between. Her tea cakes aren't highly flavored with spices or covered in decadent icing. Some may think they are short on flavor. Within the tea cake is something more important than gourmet flavor, though. These tea cakes have a legacy. Now, it's my turn to share the legend of the tea cake with my grandchildren.

Southern Tea Cakes

Yield: about 60 (2-inch) tea cakes

Preheat oven to 350°

To follow my grandmother's instructions from her unique recipe, and to mix all the ingredients together in the beginning, you must be sure to pulse the mixture until the flour is wet. After the dough is mixed, the technique is the same as my biscuit dough technique. The dough will be wet when it's turned on to a well-floured surface. Sprinkle with flour and keep working it in, adding more as needed, until the dough is no longer sticky and holds its shape. Divide the dough into four equal portions, wrap in plastic wrap, and chill at least two hours. Work with one portion of dough at a time, leaving the others in the refrigerator. The tea cakes hold their shape better if the dough remains chilled until you're ready to bake them.

4 cups all-purpose flour
2 teaspoons baking powder
1 teaspoon baking soda
2 eggs

2 cups sugar
½ cup buttermilk
1 cup (2 sticks) unsalted butter, softened
1 teaspoon vanilla

Place flour, baking powder, and soda in a large mixing bowl. Stir together.

Add remaining ingredients and mix with electric mixer. Pulse until the flour is wet. Mix with electric mixer until all ingredients are incorporated and the dough is thick and sticky. The dough gets rather thick in just a few minutes.

Turn out the dough onto a well-floured surface. Sprinkle with flour. Keep adding flour until the dough is no longer sticky and it holds its shape. I've had to add anywhere from ½ cup to 1 cup.

Divide the dough into fourths. Wrap each section with plastic wrap and chill for at least two hours up to overnight.

When ready to bake, remove one section from the refrigerator. Place dough on floured surface. Roll or pat to ½-inch thickness. Cut out tea cakes and place 1 inch apart on a baking sheet that has been greased or covered with a baking mat.

Bake at 350° for 15 minutes or until bottoms have browned slightly. Don't over bake.

Remove to a cooling rack.

Repeat with remaining dough.

It's near impossible to find wild blackberry patches these days, so I grow my own.

Blackberries from the Beginning

It started with blackberries that grew by the railroad track in Geneva, Alabama, just down the street from my grandparent's house in the Cotton Mill Village. I spent a lot of time during the summer with my grandparents in that little southeastern Alabama town. Summer in the South means insufferable heat, but it also means blackberries.

As a small child, I would pick blackberries for Granny to make cobblers, pies and jelly. She'd arm me with a bucket and an admonition, "Be particular for snakes, Shug."

During the 1960s in small town America, you could get away with sending little children alone to pick blackberries next to the railroad tracks among snakes, chiggers, and thorns the size of nickels. The bushes grew thick and the thorns were protective of the berries. Occasionally, a train would come along. I would stop picking, count the cars, and wave to the engineer on the caboose.

Blackberry summers began my love affair with food that's lasted almost six decades. I'm not sure what part of it I actually enjoyed. Was it the freedom of being responsible enough to have a job as important as picking the berries that Granny would turn into delicious cobblers and jelly? Was it the challenge of seeing how quickly I could fill my bucket? Or was it simply that I loved the smell of the berries as they cooked away in Granny's little kitchen, knowing what the end result would be?

One thing was for sure—I learned to appreciate the connection between self-sufficiency, food, and memories. The pride I felt in bringing home a full bucket of berries joined forces with the anticipation of the goodness that was soon to come out of my Granny's kitchen to produce one little girl who was just about to burst at the seams. I remember the sweet, fruity wine-like aroma that wafted throughout the house as Granny cooked the berries into jelly and cobblers. I thought the scratches from the thorns and the occasional chiggers were worth it all. But most of all, it was worth it hearing Granny sing her hymns. It was a happy time. Blackberries are the one food most closely tied to my earliest, fond food memories.

Wild blackberry bushes are hard to come by now, so I've planted my own. I never get tired of looking at them. Seeing blackberries ready for the picking is a gift to my sense of overall well-being. It just makes me happy. I don't have a railroad track running through my backyard, so I can't recreate the whole blackberry summer memory. Besides, trains no longer have cabooses and the engineers don't seem as friendly now.

Blackberry summers are the reason the blog **Syrup and Biscuits** exists. The association I made between blackberry picking and goodness soon spread to various other southern food creations that came out of my Granny's kitchen. At an early age, I was keenly aware of the power that is unleashed when people share good food. Granny's affinity for wanting to feed people infected me. If there's a cure for this infection, I hope I never find it. The love of feeding people is a gift from God that came by way of Granny. I felt like I needed to write about it.

Granny singing, the aroma of blackberries cooking away, and the promise of cobblers and jelly . . . That's what heaven will be like. Amen.

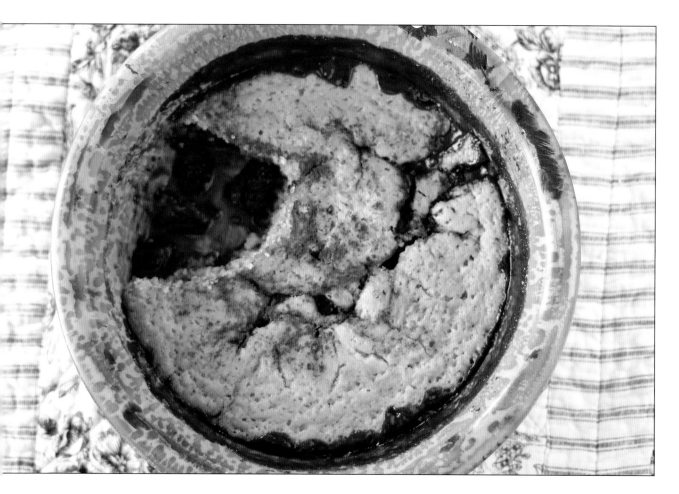

Award-Winner!

Blackberry Cobbler

Yield: 8 to 10 servings

Preheat oven to 350°

Having something that tastes unbelievably good that's easy and quick to make is a prize. In fact, this cobbler won me a prize: a Blue Ribbon.

If you're picking blackberries, then grab a handful of red ones, too. The tartness of the red berries accentuates the flavor of the cobbler. If you can't get red ones, then add a tablespoon of lemon juice.

1 stick unsalted butter
4 cups blackberries, fresh or frozen without sugar
¼ cup water
1 cup sugar
2 cups self-rising flour
2 cups milk
2 cups sugar
1 tablespoon fresh lemon juice, optional
cinnamon

Melt butter in 9-by-13-inch baking pan.

Place berries, sugar, and water in a pot and bring to a quick boil. If the berries are particularly sweet, you might not need the full cup of sugar in the berry mixture. If you're using lemon juice instead of red berries, add it to the berry mixture.

While berries are coming to a boil, mix 2 cups sugar and flour in a large bowl. Add in milk and stir well until smooth.

Pour batter over melted butter. Add hot berry mixture to the pan. Don't stir. Sprinkle with cinnamon.

Bake in a 350° oven for 30 to 45 minutes until mixture is bubbly and top has started to brown. The center will be somewhat jiggly but not loose. Let cool 15 minutes before serving.

Peach Raspberry Scones

with Peach Glaze

Yield: 16 scones

Preheat oven to 450°

I shared a recipe for savory Spinach Parmesan scones, so it seems fitting that I share a more traditional version of scones: sweet with fruits and nuts. Raspberries were on sale at the grocery store and a load of beautiful ripe peaches had just arrived. We picked up some pecans in South Georgia on our way home from the International Biscuit Festival in Knoxville, Tennessee. The availability of those three items served as inspiration for this recipe.

2 cups self–rising soft winter wheat flour
¼ cup granulated sugar plus extra to sprinkle on top
½ cup unsalted butter, cubed and chilled
1 medium ripe peach, peeled and finely diced (about ¾ cup)
½ cup fresh raspberries, frozen may be substituted
½ cup pecans, chopped
1 egg
½ cup buttermilk
Cooking oil

Add flour and sugar to a large mixing bowl and stir lightly.

Cut or rub in butter until flour resembles coarse meal.

Add peaches, raspberries, and pecans to flour mixture. Gently stir until coated with flour.

Whisk together buttermilk and egg in small bowl and pour into flour mixture. Gently stir with a large wooden spoon until the dough is wet. Don't be concerned that the raspberries break apart.

Turn out dough onto a well-floured surface. Sprinkle flour on dough and work it in, adding more as needed until the dough isn't sticky and it holds its shape.

Pat out dough into the shape of a rectangle 1-inch thick. Use a pizza cutter to cut into eight sections and each section into two triangles.

Pick up the triangles with a spatula. This helps hold its shape. Place 1 inch apart on a large baking sheet that's been greased or covered with a baking mat. Brush tops with cooking oil and sprinkle with sugar.

Bake in a 450° preheated oven for 15 minutes or until tops are golden brown and toothpick inserted comes out clean.

Remove to a cool sheet pan and glaze with Peach Glaze.

Peach Glaze

1 ripe medium peach
1–2 cups powdered sugar, depending on the amount of juice in the peach
¼–½ teaspoon apple cider vinegar

Peel peach and slice. Place slices in a fine mesh sieve over a small bowl and press out the juice with the back of a fork.

Add enough powdered sugar to make the glaze thick but pourable. If the peach is too sweet, add ¼ to ½ teaspoon apple cider vinegar to balance out the flavor.

Drizzle over the scones while they are still warm.

Peach Raspberry Scones

Bibliography

Alexander, Tamera. Tameraalexander.blogspot.net: *Beaten Biscuits, a Southern Tradition,* 2012.

Algood, Tammy. *The Complete Southern Cookbook.* Philadelphia, PA: Running Press Book Publishers, 2010.

Dull, Mrs. S.R. *Southern Cooking.* Atlanta: The Ruralist Press, 1928.

Dupree, Nathalie and Graubart, Cynthia. *Southern Biscuits.* Layton, Utah: Gibbs Smith, 2011.

Encyclopedia of Alabama
http://www.encyclopediaofalabama.org/face/Article.jsp?id=h-1333

Flynt, Wayne. *Poor But Proud: Alabama's Poor Whites.* Tuscaloosa, AL: The University of Alabama Press, 1989

Geneva Heritage Geneva Cotton Mills
http://www.genevapubliclibrary.org/genevareaper/general/Geneva%20Heritage%20Geneva%20Cotton%20Mills.pdf

Franklin County Times
http://www.franklincountytimes.com/2001/01/13/last-of-area039s-once-booming-textile-industry-closing/#

Jamestown Settlement and Yorktown Victory Center.
http://www.historyisfun.org/history-jamestown.htm

McDaniel, Rick. *Hushpuppy Nation*
http://www.hushpuppynation.com/what-did-colonists-eat-at-jamestown/

Randolph, Mary. *The Virginia Housewife: Method is the Soul of Management.* Washington, DC: printed by Way and Gideon, 1825.

Standley, Linda. Whatscookinginamerica.net: *Baking Powder – History of Baking Powder,* 2004.

Resources

Dale's Seasoning
http://www.dalesseasoning.com/

Duke's mayonnaise
http://dukesmayo.com/

Great Smoky Mountains Association stone-ground cornmeal
http://www.smokiesinformation.org/shop/stone-ground-corn-meal-2-lb-2393

King Arthur Gluten-free Baking Mix
http://www.kingarthurflour.com/shop/items/gluten-free-all-purpose-baking-mix

Lodge Cast Iron Skillets
http://www.lodgemfg.com/

MoonPie
http://moonpie.com/

Silpat Baking Mats
http://silpat.com/

Steen's 100% Pure Cane Syrup
https://www.steensyrup.com/

White Lily flour
http://www.whitelily.com/

Index

Index

Conversion Charts

METRIC AND IMPERIAL CONVERSIONS

(These conversions are rounded for convenience)

Ingredient	Cups/Tablespoons/Teaspoons	Ounces	Grams/Milliliters
Butter	1 cup=16 tablespoons= 2 sticks	8 ounces	230 grams
Cream cheese	1 tablespoon	0.5 ounce	14.5 grams
Cheese, shredded	1 cup	4 ounces	110 grams
Cornstarch	1 tablespoon	0.3 ounce	8 grams
Flour, all-purpose	1 cup/1 tablespoon	4.5 ounces/0.3 ounce	125 grams/8 grams
Flour, whole wheat	1 cup	4 ounces	120 grams
Fruit, dried	1 cup	4 ounces	120 grams
Fruits or veggies, chopped	1 cup	5 to 7 ounces	145 to 200 grams
Fruits or veggies, puréed	1 cup	8.5 ounces	245 grams
Honey, maple syrup, or corn syrup	1 tablespoon	.75 ounce	20 grams
Liquids: cream, milk, water, or juice	1 cup	8 fluid ounces	240 milliliters
Oats	1 cup	5.5 ounces	150 grams
Salt	1 teaspoon	0.2 ounces	6 grams
Spices: cinnamon, cloves, ginger, or nutmeg (ground)	1 teaspoon	0.2 ounce	5 milliliters
Sugar, brown, firmly packed	1 cup	7 ounces	200 grams
Sugar, white	1 cup/1 tablespoon	7 ounces/0.5 ounce	200 grams/12.5 grams
Vanilla extract	1 teaspoon	0.2 ounce	4 grams

OVEN TEMPERATURES

Fahrenheit	Celcius	Gas Mark
225°	110°	¼
250°	120°	½
275°	140°	1
300°	150°	2
325°	160°	3
350°	180°	4
375°	190°	5
400°	200°	6
425°	220°	7
450°	230°	8